The Red Cord of Hope

Latayne C. Scott

The Red Cord of Hope

When History Stopped for One Woman of Faith

COVENANT PUBLISHING

www.covenantpublishing.com

P.O. Box 390 · Webb City, Missouri 64870
Call toll free at 877.673.1015

Library of Congress Cataloging-in-Publication Data

Scott, Latayne Colvett, 1952-
    The red cord of hope : when history stopped for one
woman of faith /
Latayne C. Scott.
        p. cm.
    ISBN 1-892435-16-0 (pbk.)
    1. Rahab (Biblical figure) 2. Bible. O.T. Joshua II-VI
Textbooks.
    I. Title.
    BS580.R3 S38 2002
    222'.2092—dc21
                                    2002003354

Dedication

This book is lovingly dedicated to my precious son Ryan, who is my strength, and like Jesus, is my defender.

Acknowledgments

 I would like to acknowledge the unflagging support of my husband Dan and my daughter Celeste.

The role of Trinity Southwest University in Albuquerque's role in this book has been foundational and essential, for it was there that I learned ancient languages, the mechanics of Biblical semiotics (representational thinking) and the utter joy of an atmosphere of Christian collegiality. John Oller and Mike Strawn are giants upon whose shoulders I stand.

I deeply appreciate Steve Cable and Covenant Publishing for believing in this project when even I didn't have a clue how it could be done.

Helen Young and her daughters Emily Lemley, Sarah Jackson, and Marilyn Stewart were the most overt examples of faith, trust, and sweetness of spirit I have ever seen personally during the terminal illness of Marilyn. Marilyn and husband Steve Stewart have, along with the Young "girls," set a benchmark in my life for Rahabic faith.

Many readers looked over this manuscript when it was in progress, but none brought as much laughter and encouragement as Justin Brown, who sent me hilarious poems and wacky marketing ideas. Bless you, Justin!

Table of Contents

Part Two: The View out Your Window

Preface

 Who would have thought that something as frivolous as a cake would have affected my thinking so profoundly?

I stared in fascination the first time I ever saw a cake decorated with lattice frosting. Almost completely covered with an intricate web of tiny threads, the cake's round form beneath was visible, but nothing else about it. The network of hard, brittle "royal frosting" had dried to such an extent, a cake expert told me, that the frosting could be removed completely from the cake and stand independently of it.

I thought immediately of the state of our country's legal system. Its foundation, the Judeo-Christian ethic of the Bible, has been so covered over with a convoluted superstructure that the foundation is no longer even visible in many cases. In fact, most legal experts of our century would argue that the structure can stand alone and no longer needs the Bible. The more that's added, thread by thread, the less the latticework resembles what once stood below it.

But the image is even more apt when applied to what passes for Bible study in many cases. We become so entranced with the fancy decoration of Biblical truth with sweet threads of clever human thinking that we cease to pay attention to the truth that is the "form" beneath.

It is my most earnest prayer that this book will help readers want to look at the Bible itself. In the past, I have taught Biblical exegesis as the way to "get at" the truth in Scripture.

However, now I would suggest that four basic ground rules are more helpful than any set of steps.

1) No linguistic form—a comment, a paragraph, a story, or anything else—can be accurately understood when separated from its context. The story of Rahab happens in a limited continuum that begins with the promise of land to Abraham; and that's why I give some background about that promise and the people who would inherit it.

More important, however, is the greater context: the entire Bible. The Bible is the mind of God in linguistic form. He could have chosen to inform us and train us in any way He chose—pantomimes, computer chips embedded in the brain at birth, a cattle-prod mechanism activated each time we sin. But instead, He put the benefit of all His wisdom and love into our puny language. If you want to know what God likes, what impresses Him, what makes Him mad, what makes Him sad—read the whole record of His mind, the whole account of His dealings with the human race. There is no substitute for repeated and habitual reading of the whole Bible.

2) Don't use your own experiences or background or "wisdom" to judge God or Scripture. If He is who He claims to be—the Creator of the universe, perfectly fair and anxious to show mercy—then don't let your emotions or the way you think the world "works" be the standard by which you judge God and the way He deals with people. (And if He is not who He claims to be, why are you wasting time with His book? If He is who He claims to be, can you admit your lesser intelligence and when confronted with things you don't understand or like, go to a mature Christian friend or minister or book to see if there is an answer in Scripture to your dilemma?)

3) Let the Bible speak for itself whenever possible. Anytime your understanding of a difficult passage or concept is only "explained" by archaeology or psychology or some social theory—anything extraneous to the Bible—you will have undoubtedly missed the point.

Many people believe that the events and people of the Bible are so far removed from us in time that only modern study aids can explain it. But think logically with me: should we be so arrogant as to assume that only we in the 21st century can understand the Word of God? Has it just been kept in "suspended animation" until modern psychiatry or social theorists stepped in to explain it? What about the generations and cultures who have had only the Bible?

4) Operate on the assumption that God is so anxious to have you commune with His mind, the Bible, He will bless you, help you, and guide you to understanding. The role of the Holy Spirit is, after all, to guide into truth.

How This Book Is Organized

This book is divided into two sections. The first section follows the story of Rahab as it is found in the book of Joshua. In each chapter, details of the story are examined and tied to other examples of faith in the Bible.

The second section, though, is interactive in nature. It is called "The View Out Your Window," and will allow you to apply some of the lessons learned from Rahab to your own life.

You may use this book for private study; or, by using the preface and introduction as week one, you may use the lessons over a thirteen-week quarter.

Much of the teaching in this book is based on an area of theological research in which I have been involved for some ten years now and for which I am preparing a doctoral dissertation at Trinity Southwest University in Albuquerque. We call it representational thinking. It relies on some basic Biblical truths that I hope to help you see in a new light: no addition to the text, just a way of seeing it more clearly. This book is written on a "person in the pew" level. If you are interested in a more scholarly approach to the subject, feel free to write to the author in care of the publisher and I will make arrangements to give you access to a more detailed look at some of the concepts I introduce here.

May God richly bless your reading and give you abundant insight and hope in Him.

Latayne C. Scott

Scotts-on-the-Blue/ El Refugio De La Luz

January 2002

Introduction

A woman sits at a window, chin cupped in her hand, and stares into the distance.

Days—now weeks—have gone by with no word of reassurance, no hopeful words of progress, no update on a timetable. Clouds of dust eddy on the faraway horizon; and she lifts her head and strains her eyes, but it's just a capricious gust of wind stirring the bone-dry landscape beyond the distant river's banks.

She sighs.

Her gaze focuses on an object that is draped over the windowsill and that hangs onto the wall outside. The object is a *red cord,* and she idly brushes a bit of gritty dust from it, then checks for the hundredth time that day to make certain that the cord is firmly anchored by the nail she had driven those many days ago. For good measure, she glances outside the window to assure herself—again for the hundredth time—that the cord can be seen outside the window.

Like countless women before her, and millions of women after her, who have kept vigil at windows in all times and in all cultures, she sits and waits.

But she doesn't wait long in silence. Behind her, voices break into her restless reverie. The men's questions again: "How long? Any word? How can you be sure? What made you trust them? Are you sure they didn't tell you something—anything—about when?"

The women check again: "Tell us what they said, exactly what they said."

And the voices of the children: "Why can't we go outside? Nothing is happening—just like yesterday and the day before. We'll be all right. We're tired of being shut up here in this house."

And the unspoken words from everyone, tangible as those uttered: "We're scared. Everyone knows we're up against impossible odds. And the risks we're taking—we could all die."

She's scared too, but she has made her decision to wait, and she won't back down and she won't let her family— mother, father, brothers, sisters, and all their children—back down either.

The time is thousands of years ago. The place is Jericho, across from the Jordan River. And the woman is an extraordinary person. Her name is Rahab.

She is unique in history for three reasons. First of all, she is one of a very short list of women listed by name as an ancestor of Jesus. Her DNA, so to speak, contributed to His; her blood ran in His veins.

Secondly, she is on an even shorter list: those in Scripture whose recorded words explain why she would act in faith. Surely, we have many great acts of courage and faith in the Bible, but rarely do we get a glimpse of someone at the outset of faith who lists why he or she would take great risks. Like watching an edifice being built, supports and beams and rafters put into place, we can see the architecture of her faith in her words—bold, ambitious, all-or-nothing words of faith.

And thirdly, she is put on the same level, in the same category, as Abraham as concerning her faith. Yes, Abraham—the father of the faithful, the one in whose footsteps we are told to walk. "*In the same way,*" says James, the brother of Jesus in his epistle after he has talked about Abraham "was not even Rahab the prostitute considered righteous for what she did . . . ?"— acts of courage which stand as a testimony after these thousands of years of what it means to unify faith and works.

The symbol of that faith is her red cord. Against the skepticism of her family, against the dangers of doing something so likely as to cause comment and attract attention, this suspected harborer of spies hung a red flag out the window of her house for all to see.

Rahab kept her end of a bargain for salvation. She let her faith be visible, she convinced those around her to believe even when the situation looked hopeless, and most important, she knew how to wait.

And all these acts of heroism from a prostitute!

I have told the story of Rahab and her faith all over this continent and beyond, from Tennessee to Hawaii, from Washington to Oaxaca, Mexico. Everywhere I go, I recount her faith and give women a red cord of hope.

I told the story to my friend Melissa, a woman with muscular dystrophy who in her early forties was dumped in a nursing home, divorced by her husband. How do you teach hope, I asked myself, to someone who cannot do anything for herself but eat food someone else has prepared, someone who wakes from sleep and must press a call button to have a nurse turn her onto her side, an intelligent, feisty human being whose only mode of transportation is a motorized wheelchair?

> *Rahab kept her end of a bargain for salvation. She let her faith be visible, she convinced those around her to believe even when the situation looked hopeless, and most important, she knew how to wait.*

I gave Melissa a red cord, one I made myself with yarn. After I told her the story of Rahab, I assured her that Someone was coming for her. All she had to do was wait, because He's made her a promise, and He always keeps His promises. The end of the red cord might be hanging on the door of her nursing-home room, but it extends into eternity, a witness of her faith before the throne of God.

The kind of hope Rahab had was based on her faith. It wasn't just wishful thinking, it was tied directly to a promise that only God's power could fulfill. That's why hope is called an anchor for the soul, because its point of attachment is in heaven.

For that reason a red cord is included with this book. It

symbolizes promises that God has made to you personally. Such promises don't originate in your own desires or wants—but in the provision that God assures you He will give you so that you can live life here on earth triumphantly.

As we begin to understand the meaning of the kind of faith that spans across into the unseen, we too can learn how to trust as Rahab did. Rahab, you will see, knew of God's power. Nothing of doctrine, nothing of worship. From that raw exercise of dynamic, explosive ability He'd demonstrated at the Red Sea, she concluded that He was the kind of God she wanted to serve. So she extracted a promise from His representatives.

We will never know how each decision of faith—or faithlessness—will affect generations after us.

None of us will live long enough to see the long-term effects of our faith on our children's children's children. We will never know how each decision of faith—or faithlessness—will affect generations after us. How marvelous the Bible is—it lets us see how one woman's faith can affect people decades, centuries, even thousands of years later. In the Bible, we can see the long-term effects of sin and righteousness on individuals and on their progeny they never lived to see.

What did Rahab learn to do? What skill did she have that we can imitate so that we can know our heritage for coming generations will stand in faith?

She knew how to hold on in difficult circumstances—to cling to her red cord of hope. Most importantly, she knew not just to wait, but how to wait.

For Rahab, her faith was irrevocably bound together with the tangible symbol of it, the red cord.

As was true thousands of years ago and even to today in the Hebrew language, the word for hope or expectation, *tiqwah*, is also the word for cord.

Part One:

Rahab's Story

Chapter 1

The Story Before the Story

 When you have completed reading this chapter, go to the "Chapter One Response" in the second section of this book, "The View out Your Window."

Rahab's Story in the Old Testament

To get the background of the story of Rahab, we have to go back to the time, thousands of years before Christ, that God gave a promise to Abraham. He swore to Abraham that He would not only give that man a son, from whom a mighty nation would spring, but that He would also provide a homeland for them. Abraham as well as many generations of Israelites lived and died without ever possessing that homeland, but they lived and died in faith convinced that this country was a coming reality.

During a time of famine that occurred during the youth of Joseph, Abraham's great-grandson, God sent His people away from that region. In Egypt the Israelites were saved from the immediate threat of starvation, but as they continued to live in Egypt, over a four-hundred-year period they became enslaved and cried out continually to God for help.

That brings us up to the time that Moses led the children of Israel out of Egypt. Anyone who has seen the movie, *The Ten Commandments*, knows that after the ten plagues, Pharaoh finally relented and let the people go. Then he changed his mind and sent soldiers after them, and God performed yet another miracle, the crossing of the Red Sea, an act that simultaneously rescued them and killed their pursuers.

Within just 72 hours, those people who had seen all those miracles were grumbling and threatening to go back to the land of slavery because they didn't trust that same God to be able to "spread a table" for them in the wilderness. Of course He did just exactly that, with daily manna and enough water for the millions of people. Thus fortified, the people marched resolutely to Sinai, which with the Lord's direction they reached in about three months—with plenty of food and water all along the way. There on the mountain Moses received the Ten Commandments.

The Lord, who is jealous of His identity and did not want to be remembered as a cow, was angry; and many of the unfaithful were put to death over that incident.

However, during the time he was up there listening to the Lord, the people lost heart and built a gold statue of a calf and declared that a bovine had led them out of Egypt. The Lord, who is jealous of His identity and did not want to be remembered as a cow, was angry; and many of the unfaithful were put to death over that incident. Moses broke the tablets and was called back to the mountain—this time for forty days—to hear the voice of God again and to receive the same commandments on newly-carved stones, which he brought down to the people.

From the instructions he'd received on the mountain, Moses directed the building of a portable building, the Tabernacle, to house the presence of the Lord. From that point on, the people would look to a cloud that hung over that tent of meeting, to know if they should remain camped or if they would move on to another spot in the desert.

In the midst of constant griping, backstabbing, and rebelliousness, the unruly group was led in a few short months to a place in the desert of Paran, at Kadesh Barnea. At that point, the nearly two million people were only about 50 miles from the borders of the land they'd been promised those hundreds of years before.

Moses sent twelve spies into the land, and they brought back a report of incredible richness—and incredible danger. Two of the spies, Joshua and Caleb, depended on what the Lord had said about their eventual success while the other ten not only acted on their fears, but also convinced all the other hundreds of thousands of adult Israelites that it couldn't be done no matter what God had said about the matter.

God's patience with them finally ran out. No adult, He declared, would live to enter the promised land. For nearly four more decades, the Israelites would live and inevitably die often literally within sight of a land they would never enjoy. The next nearly 40 years were spent in camping out, gathering manna, and burying the dead. During the last year in the desert, the young adults learned the art of war as they defeated several local kings at the border of the promised land.

When we arrive at the events of Joshua chapter 2, Moses has died and has passed the reins of leadership to Joshua, who along with Caleb are the only adults who had experienced the crossing of the Red Sea who remain alive. A nation of orphans, a new generation of hundreds of thousands of people, are camped in dry, dusty Shittim, which means "acacia trees," near a low mountain range. Between the mountains and the enormous and powerful walled city of Jericho was the Jordan River, raging and churning at flood stage. We join the story as Joshua is dispatching two young men to spy out Jericho.

Joshua 2:1-24

Then Joshua son of Nun secretly sent two spies from Shittim. "Go, look over the land," he said, "especially Jericho." So they went and entered the house of a prostitute named Rahab and stayed there. The king of Jericho was told, "Look! Some of the Israelites have come here tonight to spy out the land." So the king of Jericho sent this message to Rahab: "Bring out the men who came to you and entered your house, because they have come to spy out the whole land."

But the woman had taken the two men and hidden them. She said, "Yes, the men came to me, but I did not know where they had come from. At dusk, when it was time to close the city gate, the men left. I don't know which way they went. Go after them quickly. You may catch up with them."

Persuasive faith knows facts about God's power and uses them to build faith in others.

(But she had taken them up to the roof and hidden them under the stalks of flax she had laid out on the roof.) So the men set out in pursuit of the spies on the road that leads to the fords of the Jordan, and as soon as the pursuers had gone out, the gate was shut.

It is at this point that Rahab, who has become a traitor to her countrymen, disobedient to her king, and has lied for these spies (more about that later), thinks to bargain for her actions. But before she does that, she tells the spies about the emotional climate of the city and begins to show why she has taken these enormous risks.

Before the spies lay down for the night, she went up on the roof and said to them, "I know that the LORD has given this land to you and that a great fear of you has fallen on us, so that all who live in this country are melting in fear because of you. We have heard how the LORD dried up the water of the Red Sea for you when you came out of Egypt, and what you did to Sihon and Og, the two kings of the Amorites east of the Jordan, whom you completely destroyed. When we heard of it, our hearts melted and everyone's courage failed because of you, for the LORD your God is God in heaven above and on the earth below."

2:8-11

She wants to be on the team that will win, the team with the most powerful God. So she presses her advantage.

Now then, please swear to me by the LORD that you will show kindness to my family, because I have shown kindness to you. Give me a sure sign that you will spare the lives of my father and mother, my brothers and sisters, and all who belong to them, and that you will save us from death.

2:12-13

The men agree, with two conditions, the first of which is that she cannot tell anyone what the spies are doing.

> *"Our lives for your lives!" the men assured her. "If you don't tell what we are doing, we will treat you kindly and faithfully when the LORD gives us the land."*
> *So she let them down by a rope through the window, for the house she lived in was part of the city wall. Now she had said to them, "Go to the hills so the pursuers will not find you. Hide yourselves there three days until they return, and then go on your way."*
> 2:15-16

Then the spies add another condition—Rahab must persuade all her loved ones to stay in her brothel with her.

> *The men said to her, "This oath you made us swear will not be binding on us unless, when we enter the land, you have tied this scarlet cord in the window through which you let us down, and unless you have brought your father and mother, your brothers and all your family into your house. If anyone goes outside your house into the street, his blood will be on his own head; we will not be responsible. As for anyone who is in the house with you, his blood will be on our head if a hand is laid on him. But if you tell what we are doing, we will be released from the oath you made us swear."*
> 2:17-20

The symbol of their agreement is hardly an inconspicuous one: She must hang the bright cord out the window of a wall of the most powerful—and oft-visited—city in the world. But she doesn't hesitate and does it immediately.

> *"Agreed," she replied. "Let it be as you say." So she sent them away and they departed. And she tied the scarlet cord in the window.*
> *When they left, they went into the hills and stayed there three days, until the pursuers had searched all along the road and returned without finding them. Then the two men started back. They went down out of the hills, forded the river and came to Joshua son of Nun and told him everything that had happened to them. They said to Joshua, "The LORD has surely given the*

whole land into our hands; all the people are melting in fear because of us."

2:21-24

During the next few days the people prepare themselves for crossing the raging Jordan River.

Joshua 3:1-17

Early in the morning Joshua and all the Israelites set out from Shittim and went to the Jordan, where they camped before crossing over. After three days the officers went throughout the camp, giving orders to the people: "When you see the ark of the covenant of the LORD your God, and the priests, who are Levites, carrying it, you are to move out from your positions and follow it. Then you will know which way to go, since you have never been this way before. But keep a distance of about a thousand yards between you and the ark; do not go near it."

Joshua told the people, "Consecrate yourselves, for tomorrow the LORD will do amazing things among you."

Joshua said to the priests, "Take up the ark of the covenant and pass on ahead of the people." So they took it up and went ahead of them.

And the LORD said to Joshua, "Today I will begin to exalt you in the eyes of all Israel, so they may know that I am with you as I was with Moses. Tell the priests who carry the ark of the covenant: 'When you reach the edge of the Jordan's waters, go and stand in the river.'"

Joshua said to the Israelites, "Come here and listen to the words of the LORD your God. This is how you will know that the living God is among you and that he will certainly drive out before you the Canaanites, Hittites, Hivites, Perizzites, Girgashites, Amorites and Jebusites. See, the ark of the covenant of the LORD of all the earth will go into the Jordan ahead of you. Now then, choose twelve men from the tribes of Israel, one from each tribe. And as soon as the priests who carry the ark of the LORD—the LORD of all the earth—set foot in the Jordan, its waters flowing downstream will be cut off and stand up in a heap."

So when the people broke camp to cross the Jordan, the priests carrying the ark of the covenant went ahead of them. Now the Jordan is at flood stage all during harvest. Yet as soon as the priests who carried the ark reached the Jordan and their feet touched the water's edge, the water from upstream stopped flowing. It piled up in a heap a great distance away, at a town called Adam in the vicinity of Zarethan, while the water flowing down to the Sea of the Arabah (the Salt Sea) was completely cut off. So the people crossed over opposite Jericho. The priests who carried the ark of the covenant of the LORD stood firm on dry ground in the middle of the Jordan, while all Israel passed by until the whole nation had completed the crossing on dry ground.

Although God had just done a repeat performance, so to speak, of the crossing of the Red Sea, He wanted to leave a symbol of that event for people of coming generations to contemplate. So the twelve stones are piled up and instructions given concerning their significance.

Joshua 4:1-24

When the whole nation had finished crossing the Jordan, the LORD said to Joshua, "Choose twelve men from among the people, one from each tribe, and tell them to take up twelve stones from the middle of the Jordan from right where the priests stood and to carry them over with you and put them down at the place where you stay tonight."

So Joshua called together the twelve men he had appointed from the Israelites, one from each tribe, and said to them, "Go over before the ark of the LORD your God into the middle of the Jordan. Each of you is to take up a stone on his shoulder, according to the number of the tribes of the Israelites, to serve as a sign among you. In the future, when your children ask you, 'What do these stones mean?' tell them that the flow of the Jordan was cut off before the ark of the covenant of the LORD. When it crossed the Jordan, the waters of the Jordan were cut off. These stones are

to be a memorial to the people of Israel forever."

So the Israelites did as Joshua commanded them. They took twelve stones from the middle of the Jordan, according to the number of the tribes of the Israelites, as the LORD had told Joshua; and they carried them over with them to their camp, where they put them down. Joshua set up the twelve stones that had been in the middle of the Jordan at the spot where the priests who carried the ark of the covenant had stood. And they are there to this day.

Now the priests who carried the ark remained standing in the middle of the Jordan until everything the LORD had commanded Joshua was done by the people, just as Moses had directed Joshua. The people hurried over, and as soon as all of them had crossed, the ark of the LORD and the priests came to the other side while the people watched. The men of Reuben, Gad and the half-tribe of Manasseh crossed over, armed, in front of the Israelites, as Moses had directed them. About forty thousand armed for battle crossed over before the LORD to the plains of Jericho for war.

That day the LORD exalted Joshua in the sight of all Israel; and they revered him all the days of his life, just as they had revered Moses.

Then the LORD said to Joshua, "Command the priests carrying the ark of the Testimony to come up out of the Jordan."

So Joshua commanded the priests, "Come up out of the Jordan." And the priests came up out of the river carrying the ark of the covenant of the LORD. No sooner had they set their feet on the dry ground than the waters of the Jordan returned to their place and ran at flood stage as before.

On the tenth day of the first month the people went up from the Jordan and camped at Gilgal on the eastern border of Jericho. And Joshua set up at Gilgal the twelve stones they had taken out of the Jordan. He said to the Israelites, "In the future when your descendants ask their fathers, 'What do these stones mean?' tell them, 'Israel crossed the Jordan on dry ground.' For the LORD your God dried up the Jordan before you until you had crossed over. The LORD your God did to the Jordan just what he had done to the Red Sea when he dried it up before us until we had crossed over. He did this so that all the peoples of the earth might know that the hand of the LORD is powerful and so that you might always fear the LORD your God."

Obviously the nearby city of Jericho and even neighboring kingdoms are scared silly by a group of people who can cause a flooded river to stop in its tracks. But if they expected an immediate invasion, their nerves must have been further frazzled by the Israelite's stopping to circumcise all the adult males and to re-institute the feast of the Passover.

Joshua 5:1-15

Now when all the Amorite kings west of the Jordan and all the Canaanite kings along the coast heard how the LORD had dried up the Jordan before the Israelites until we had crossed over, their hearts melted and they no longer had the courage to face the Israelites.

At that time the LORD said to Joshua, "Make flint knives and circumcise the Israelites again." So Joshua made flint knives and circumcised the Israelites at Gibeath Haaraloth.

Now this is why he did so: All those who came out of Egypt— all the men of military age—died in the desert on the way after leaving Egypt. All the people that came out had been circumcised, but all the people born in the desert during the journey from Egypt had not. The Israelites had moved about in the desert forty years until all the men who were of military age when they left Egypt had died, since they had not obeyed the LORD. For the LORD had sworn to them that they would not see the land that he had solemnly promised their fathers to give us, a land flowing with milk and honey. So he raised up their sons in their place, and these were the ones Joshua circumcised. They were still uncircumcised because they had not been circumcised on the way. And after the whole nation had been circumcised, they remained where they were in camp until they were healed.

Then the LORD said to Joshua, "Today I have rolled away the

reproach of Egypt from you." So the place has been called Gilgal to this day.

On the evening of the fourteenth day of the month, while camped at Gilgal on the plains of Jericho, the Israelites cele-brated the Passover. The day after the Passover, that very day, they ate some of the produce of the land: unleavened bread and roasted grain. The manna stopped the day after they ate this food from the land; there was no longer any manna for the Israelites, but that year they ate of the produce of Canaan.

At this time a rather peculiar incident occurs when Joshua is confronted by an enigmatic divine Being (more about that later, too.)

Now when Joshua was near Jericho, he looked up and saw a man standing in front of him with a drawn sword in his hand. Joshua went up to him and asked, "Are you for us or for our enemies?"

"Neither," he replied, "but as commander of the army of the LORD I have now come." Then Joshua fell facedown to the ground in reverence, and asked him, "What message does my LORD have for his servant?"

The commander of the LORD's army replied, "Take off your sandals, for the place where you are standing is holy." And Joshua did so.

Now all the preparations are done. Jericho has gone into siege mode, and must have braced its collective heart when it saw the Ark of the Covenant and its accompanying priests and armed guard.

Joshua 6:1-25

Now Jericho was tightly shut up because of the Israelites. No one went out and no one came in.

Then the LORD said to Joshua, "See, I have delivered Jericho into your hands, along with its king and its fighting men. March around the city once with all the armed men. Do this for six days. Have seven priests carry trumpets of rams' horns in front of the ark. On the seventh day, march around the city seven times, with the priests blowing the trumpets. When you hear them sound a long blast on the trumpets, have all the people give a loud shout; then the wall of the city will collapse and the people will go up, every man straight in."

So Joshua son of Nun called the priests and said to them, "Take up the ark of the covenant of the LORD and have seven priests carry trumpets in front of it." And he ordered the people, "Advance! March around the city, with the armed guard going ahead of the ark of the LORD."

When Joshua had spoken to the people, the seven priests carrying the seven trumpets before the LORD went forward, blowing their trumpets, and the ark of the LORD's covenant followed them. The armed guard marched ahead of the priests who blew the trumpets, and the rear guard followed the ark. All this time the trumpets were sounding. But Joshua had commanded the people, "Do not give a war cry, do not raise your voices, do not say a word until the day I tell you to shout. Then shout!" So he had the ark of the LORD carried around the city, circling it once. Then the people returned to camp and spent the night there.

Joshua got up early the next morning and the priests took up the ark of the LORD. The seven priests carrying the seven trumpets went forward, marching before the ark of the LORD and blowing the trumpets. The armed men went ahead of them and the rear guard followed the ark of the LORD, while the trumpets kept sounding. So on the second day they marched around the city once and returned to the camp. They did this for six days.

On the seventh day, they got up at daybreak and marched around the city seven times in the same manner, except that on that day they circled the city seven times. The seventh time around, when the priests sounded the trumpet blast, Joshua commanded the people, "Shout! For the LORD has given you the city! The city and all that is in it are to be devoted to the LORD. Only Rahab the prostitute and all who are with her in her house shall be spared, because she hid the spies we sent.

But keep away from the devoted things, so that you will not bring about your own destruction by taking any of them. Otherwise you will make the camp of Israel liable to destruction and bring trouble on it. All the silver and gold and the articles of bronze and iron are sacred to the LORD and must go into his treasury."

When the trumpets sounded, the people shouted, and at the sound of the trumpet, when the people gave a loud shout, the wall collapsed; so every man charged straight in, and they took the city. They devoted the city to the LORD and destroyed with the sword every living thing in it—men and women, young and old, cattle, sheep and donkeys.

Only one part of the wall is not in ruins. One small section with a red cord hanging out of a window still stands above the smoking ruins, and Rahab and her family are rescued from that spot.

Joshua said to the two men who had spied out the land, "Go into the prostitute's house and bring her out and all who belong to her, in accordance with your oath to her." So the young men who had done the spying went in and brought out Rahab, her father and mother and brothers and all who belonged to her. They brought out her entire family and put them in a place outside the camp of Israel.

Then they burned the whole city and everything in it, but they put the silver and gold and the articles of bronze and iron into the treasury of the LORD's house. But Joshua spared Rahab the prostitute, with her family and all who belonged to her, because she hid the men Joshua had sent as spies to Jericho— and she lives among the Israelites to this day.

Rahab

Your bed of short-lived pleasures
Your years of broken promises of commitment
Your spilled bottles of hope
Your façade of beauty smeared over hideous reality
Your hole in the wall hit-and-run—
You shameful,
You worthless,
You wretched,
You low-life—
Who because of a pindrop of faith
In the power of a God
You had only heard rumors about—
Are now crowned to commune above your class.
Dear wretched, worthless whore,
Now feast on the eternal delight
That Jehovah truly rewards
All
Who trust Him.

—Celeste Scott

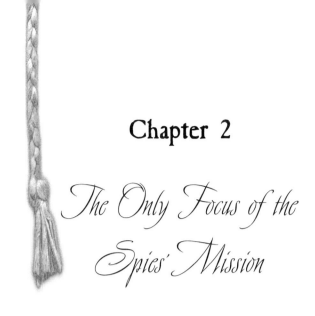

Chapter 2

The Only Focus of the Spies' Mission

 In this, and all subsequent chapters, we will examine in detail the story of Rahab's faith. We will begin again at the beginning, when Joshua first sends the two spies to Jericho.

> Then Joshua son of Nun secretly sent two spies from Shittim. "Go, look over the land," he said, "especially Jericho."
>
> Joshua 2:1a

Why only two spies for such an important spy mission? The last time that a spy team had been sent into the promised land, there had been twelve—sort of a democratic representation of the twelve tribes of Israel. But one of the bitter lessons of that experience had been that only two had been able to believe God's power was greater than the strength of the enemy they faced. The other ten, in fact, had managed to dishearten and discourage over six million people.[1] It would have been better if they'd never gone; better if two men of faith alone had brought back the report that was later so twisted by ten men of fear.

Now that you've read the entire story of Rahab from beginning to end, you can see the irony in the first statement in the account. Joshua sends two young men into the promised land. We don't know exactly how they got across the flooded Jordan River and what other sites they scouted out on this reconnaissance trip, but their expedition is near the end when they enter the enormous and powerful walled city of Jericho.

The two spies were sent to Jericho for only one purpose: to search out and identify the one person of faith in that city so she would be spared.

Here's the irony. Now that you know how Jericho was defeated, what tactical knowledge did the spies get on this trip which Joshua and they needed to know? Did any knowledge of the thickness of the wall make any difference on that seventh circuit on the seventh day when the ram's horns blew? Did the kinds or number of Jericho's arsenal force make any real difference in the long run? Did it really matter in the end how many soldiers Jericho had?

So you begin to see where the irony comes in. The two spies were sent to Jericho for only one purpose: to search out and identify the one person of faith in that city so she would be spared.

Think of it! God held up human history, in the most amazing conquest ever recorded in history, to alert and protect just one person of faith!

It wasn't the first time in human history that God had done exactly this. Long ago, God had announced to His servant Abraham that He intended to destroy the cities of Sodom and Gomorrah. In an astonishing interlude found in Genesis chapter 18,[2] God holds up the whole process while Abraham "bargains down" the God of the universe to the puny sum of ten. If just ten people can be found in Sodom, conceded God, then He would not destroy the whole city. But of course there weren't even ten there, and the ones who were rescued—Lot and his family—had to be dragged out by the hand by angels.

Nonetheless, God is anxiously looking over the world in every generation, searching for those who are truly devoted to Him, and He won't spare any of His resources—people, wealth, even time itself—to find them: in 2 Chronicles 16:9, it says that "the eyes of the Lord range throughout the earth to strengthen those whose hearts are fully committed to Him."

I emphasize time as a resource because of what Matthew 24:22 says. In describing a coming time of great tribulation and suffering, Jesus says that for "the elect," even time itself

36

will be shortened. God will do anything to promote faith in those who are seeking Him. As the story of Rahab shows, He even held up an invasion extra days just for her.

Was Rahab a Prostitute?

So they went and entered the house of a prostitute named Rahab and stayed there.

2:1b

I once sat in a Sunday school class where a teacher laboriously brought in supposed archaeological evidence to try to prove that Rahab wasn't a prostitute. Because the word translated from the Hebrew can mean either prostitute or innkeeper, this teacher went to great lengths to try to show that this great woman of faith had an unspotted past.

But there are several compelling reasons we have to believe that she was indeed a woman of "ill repute."

First of all, when Rahab is referred to in the New Testament, there's no problem with a double meaning for the word. In James,[3] she is called a "porne." That is the root word of the English word pornography; and what could have been questioned about the Hebrew is unmistakable in the Greek.

Secondly, just because she was a direct ancestor of Jesus doesn't mean she had to be sinless. If you look in the genealogy of Jesus where the name of Rahab appears,[4] you will also find the names of Tamar[5] (who dressed as a prostitute to lure the father of her dead husband to have sex with her so she'd have a legal heir in his line) and "the wife of Uriah," or Bathsheba,[6] who had sex with king David while married to another man. Also in the list of Jesus' progenitors were idol worshipers, murderers, and thieves.

Thirdly, it is limiting God—and unfaithful to Scripture—to even imply that God only works with "good" people. In fact, if you see how Jesus related to sinful women, you will see that He went out of His way to reward them for faith. He was deeply touched, for instance, when a notoriously promiscuous woman sneaked into a banquet He was attending and wept over His feet, drying them with her hair and then anointing

Even a prostitute like Rahab who was outside the bloodline of Abraham's promise could be saved because of her faith.

them with fragrant ointment.[7]

Even though Jesus' primary mission on earth was to teach the distant descendants of those who conquered Jericho, He nonetheless was impressed with another woman who was outside of that national heritage, an unnamed Syrophoenician woman in Mark 7. When she asked Him to heal her daughter, He told this Greek woman that He needed to use His time and efforts toward the Jews: "First let the children eat all they want," he told her, "for it is not right to take the children's bread and toss it to their dogs."[8]

Such a statement didn't "put off" this woman of faith—she respectfully reminded Him that even dogs under the table get crumbs. It was on the basis of this kind of faith, Jesus said, for such a reply, that He healed her daughter immediately.

Even a prostitute like Rahab who was outside the bloodline of Abraham's promise could be saved because of her faith. Even a woman from an idolatrous country like Moab could become the grandmother of King David even when she had been a widowed welfare recipient—for that is exactly what Ruth was when Boaz married her.[9] And a Cushite man's faith caused him to be saved when the whole holy city of Jerusalem was sacked around him.[10]

It's a good thing, in fact, that God has always placed faith above lineage—because the vast majority of Christians from Paul's time on have been "foreigners" as regards an Israelite bloodline, and even more in our hopeless, alienated souls[11] and yet Jesus saves us just as if we were the children of the conquerors of Jericho.

Rahab was outside of that promise when she was born, but God placed her inside the promise when she acted in faith in Him. Faith was like an adoption certificate for this woman who became part of God's family at that moment.

But what about her past? Her years of selling her body, as we will see later, would have certainly affected her credibility in her community and with her family. Here is a woman who may or may not have been a shrewd businesswoman but who was identified by all who knew her by her line of work. Yet God didn't judge her on the basis of her past sins, but on her faith in Him. The events that had happened in her life were facts. But God chose to represent them as something else when she acted for Him.

How to Re-Represent Our Past

A good example of how this re-representing by God works is found in Zechariah 3. Joshua (a different man from the account in Judges) the high priest was standing before the angel of the Lord and Satan stood there accusing him. The Lord rebuked Satan and told him that the Lord had chosen Jerusalem and the nation of Israel that Joshua symbolized, and that the Lord had snatched Joshua back from the fire of destruction like a man would grab a burning stick out of a firepit.

But Joshua stood before the Lord in filthy clothes, a symbol of how the nation had sinned and brought disgrace on itself. Nothing Joshua could do for himself would help. The Lord commanded the angel to take off Joshua's soiled clothing. "See, I have taken away your sin, and I will put rich garments on you."[12]

Here's how we deal with past sins: The Lord doesn't deny that they happened. We don't try to pretend they didn't either. Those are facts.

However, we can choose to represent them in one of two ways.

We can represent them according to our own preferences as how to think and talk about them. We may try to gloss them over and say, "I'm only human, and everybody makes mistakes, and I'm just not going to take responsibility for something to make myself feel bad." Or we may choose to dwell on them, let them "mark" us and bear their guilt, shame, and anger. Before we belonged to the Lord, those were our only two options for dealing with the facts: ignore and gloss over past sins or let bad past experiences formulate our negative thoughts about ourselves and others—as well as the God

God has only one representation for the facts of past sins: "I the LORD remember them no more."

who would have witnessed those events.

But someone who belongs to Christ doesn't have those options. God has only one representation for the facts of past sins: "I the LORD remember them no more."[13]

Whose representations do we choose about our painful past? Do we rely on our own representations of our memories of them and the associated feelings?

Or do we, by an act of the will, choose to accept God's representations of them?:

That God will bring good out of every circumstance, good or bad, for a believer[14]

That Christ's blood continually—like a windshield washer—washes away our sins[15]

That He personally bears our sins so we don't have to[16]

That He throws our sins into the depths of the sea[17]

That He even chooses to completely forget our sins as if they'd never happened[18]

But it's hard to accept God's representations of our past when we have such vivid memories, isn't it?

Paul certainly understood this. Even though he was an apostle and had seen Jesus personally, had heard His voice, Paul still must have remembered the days when he had broken into people's homes and dragged Christians out to be put to death. Every time that Paul faced a child whom he'd orphaned, a woman he'd made a widow, his heart must have ached. He didn't deny the past facts, but by an act of the will he chose to represent them not according to his own guilt and pain, but according to how God saw him now.

"Christ Jesus came into the world to save sinners," Paul said "—of whom I am the worst. But for that very reason I was shown mercy so that in me, the worst of sinners, Christ Jesus might display his unlimited patience as an example for those who would believe on him and receive eternal life."[19]

Just as Paul was an example of someone with a past full of horrible, shameful facts who chose to represent them according to God's assessments, so was Rahab an example of an Old Testament woman who did the same.

And how does God view the woman who was a prostitute at the very moment she did the most heroic thing of her life? She is listed in Hebrews 11, a chapter known as "the roll call of the faithful," as one of the few, the proud, the faithful.

Chapter 3

Sex, Lies, and Victorious Faith

The king of Jericho was told, "Look! Some of the Israelites have come here tonight to spy out the land." So the king of Jericho sent this message to Rahab: "Bring out the men who came to you and entered your house, because they have come to spy out the whole land."

But the woman had taken the two men and hidden them. She said, "Yes, the men came to me, but I did not know where they had come from. At dusk, when it was time to close the city gate, the men left. I don't know which way they went. Go after them quickly. You may catch up with them." (But she had taken them up to the roof and hidden them under the stalks of flax she had laid out on the roof.) So the men set out in pursuit of the spies on the road that leads to the fords of the Jordan, and as soon as the pursuers had gone out, the gate was shut.

Joshua 2:2-7

It is at this point in Rahab's story that the issue of the lie she told to protect the men must be dealt with. The matter is a thorny one, for unlike her status of prostitute that Scripture just mentions and dismisses, her lie is actually commended.

First of all, in Hebrews 11, Rahab's actions are shown to be of faith. But specifically, the approved action was that of harboring the spies.

"By faith the prostitute Rahab, because she welcomed the spies, was not killed with those who were disobedient."[20]

Her action of welcoming them included hiding them and telling a lie about where they were. This is made even more plain in James chapter 2. In this passage that shows that faith alone is dead if not accompanied by deeds, James shows that Abraham's faith was not complete until he joined it with action—his willingness to sacrifice his son. *"In the same way,"* says James, "was not even Rahab the prostitute considered righteous for what she did . . . ." [emphasis added].

Rahab is commended, in the only two passages in the New Testament that mention her, for telling a lie.

And what exactly does James say she did? What were the actions that completed her faith? The first was "she gave lodging to the spies."

But the second was that she "sent them [the spies] off in a different direction." A different direction than what? Than the direction and manner she told the king's men they had gone. In other words, Rahab is commended, in the only two passages in the New Testament that mention her, for telling a lie.

Now, the Bible is quite plain in its condemnation of bearing false witness and dishonesty in any form. However, we can learn an important principle from this and one other clear Biblical example of lying, both of which cases are commended by God.

The other instance is found in Exodus chapter 1, when the king of Egypt commanded the Hebrew midwives Shiphrah and Puah that when they attended Israelite women in labor, they should kill all the newborn males and let the females live.

"The midwives, however, feared God and did not do what the king of Egypt had told them to do; they let the boys live. Then the king of Egypt summoned the midwives and asked them, 'Why have you done this? Why have you let the boys live?'

"The midwives answered Pharaoh, 'Hebrew women are not like Egyptian women; they are vigorous and give birth before the midwives arrive.'

"So God was kind to the midwives and the people increased and became even more numerous. And because the midwives feared God, he gave them families of their own."[21]

From the example of Rahab and that of the midwives we can see that there are indeed circumstances when God would honor a believer telling a lie. But those circumstances are very, very narrow. They would have to include the following three elements that are common to both stories: disobeying a command that counters the will of God, given by an unrighteous authority; a life-or-death situation; and the willingness of the person telling the lie to put her own life on the line if discovered.[22]

It is this last point for which we should most honor Rahab, I believe. Not only did she show kindness to the spies, she put herself in immediate personal danger. Given the climate of near-panic that had gripped the city, there can be little doubt that she would have been killed without a second thought if it had come to light that she had become a traitor to her own people.

It is at this point, too, that another issue should be at least briefly addressed: that of the role of patriotism in the life of a Christian. Though American citizens and those of other democracies should be grateful to God for life in countries where they can practice religious freedom, each believer must be willing to distinguish clearly between obedience to earthly authorities as commanded in Scripture,[23] and obedience to God when those authorities command something which God forbids.[24]

Rahab's History Lesson

Before the spies lay down for the night, she went up on the roof and said to them, "I know that the LORD has given this land to you and that a great fear of you has fallen on us, so that all who live in this country are melting in fear because of you. We have heard how the LORD dried up the water of the Red Sea for you when you came out of Egypt, and what you did to Sihon and Og, the two kings of the Amorites east of the Jordan, whom you completely destroyed. When we heard of it, our hearts melted and everyone's courage failed because of you . . . ."

2:8-11a

Rahab's knowledge of the last forty years of Hebrew history is astonishing, because it closely resembles what the Bible tells us. Though we know many details about the first two years (those which followed the crossing of the Red Sea) and the events of the fortieth year, there are almost no Biblical details about the 37 years in between.[25] We have little more than a listing of some 40 places[26] where they pitched tents, gathered manna, and buried the dead.

These Israelites were unstoppable, it seemed.

But in that fortieth year, the action began to really ramp up. Rahab mentions that the Israelite army had defeated Sihon and Og,[27] two powerful kings east of the Jordan. Beginning in that fortieth year, many additional important events took place in Israelite history. The Canaanite tribe led by a king named Arad attacked Israel and God helped them defeat this tribe,[28] the Midianites were defeated[29] and the attempts by the king of Moab were thwarted.[30] A new census was taken and in numbers that nearly matched the number of fighting men who had left Egypt and had died, over 600,000 adult men formed a standing army.[31] It was therefore this army, with those victories under its belt, that had the entire city of Jericho senseless with fear.

Where would Rahab have gotten the stories she knew about the Red Sea? The defeating of neighboring kings Sihon and Og was probably big news in that area, brought to the great trade center of Jericho by passing merchants, soldiers who had escaped or defected, and other travelers to the city. Undoubtedly such a string of decisive military victories carried out by a group of nomads who'd been in the desert for four decades would have caught all the military powers of the area off guard, and gotten the attention of Jericho as well. And then people would have started remembering the tales that had been told about how the firstborn children of all the mighty nation of Egypt, from the crown prince on down to the poorest laborer's child, had died the night those same nomads had left the country to cross dryshod through a seabed that had suddenly swallowed up Pharaoh himself and his army as well . . . .

Putting those stories together with the recent coups of their neighbors was enough to scare anybody, from the king of Jericho down to the prostitute living on the city wall. These Israelites were unstoppable, it seemed.

But there was a dark side to the last year of desert dwelling for the Israelites, events of which Rahab was probably unaware. By the end of the fortieth year all the people who had nearly four decades before rebelled at Kadesh Barnea—those who had accused God of taking them out into the desert just to kill them—had their bodies covered over in the ceaselessly shifting sands of the bleak desert. But tragically, their sons and daughters had fallen back into their fathers' sins. Just months—just days—from receiving the promised land, they blew it again—and again.

Now, back at Kadesh after 38 years of wandering, the people rose up, just as their parents had done against Moses and Aaron, complaining about the lack of water and accusing their leaders of bringing them and their livestock to the desert to die.[32] It was there that Moses finally lost his temper, struck the rock to bring water, and learned the bitter lesson of the holiness of God. Later that year, the people grew impatient again, again accused Moses of bringing them there to die, and complained against the manna as "miserable food." For that, God sent them venomous snakes whose deadly bites were only assuaged by the sight of a bronze snake hung on a pole,[33] but only after many died.

But the worst was yet to come. The people got right to the borders of the land. (They knew they were right at the border—Moses gave them the boundaries.[34]) They knew they were at the end of the forty years too when they arrived at Moab—in Shittim from which the spies that would encounter Rahab were dispatched. It was there that the men began to engage in the pagan fertility rites of the Canaanites, and "the people ate and bowed down before these gods."[35] A fed-up God demanded that all the leaders of this insanity be killed.

It's not as if they hadn't known that they were on the verge of redemption. After all, when the ten spies from the first spy party had managed to whip their brethren into a state of fear and rebellion and God had told them they would all die in the desert, He had put a time limit on it. "Your children will be shepherds here for forty years," God told them, "suffering for your unfaithfulness, until the last of your bodies lies in the desert. For forty years—one year for each of the forty days you explored the land . . . "[36]

So close to redemption! And right across the line from the land they'd trudged through sand for forty years to inherit, 24,000 men died for idolatry!

Perhaps if Rahab had known that, she would have had even more fear for the God of the Israelites. She knew only His power against His enemies, but apparently never suspected that the people He'd so blessed with His power could ever dream of rebellion and incur the same judgment as their enemies.

A Confession of Faith

> . . . for the LORD your God is God in heaven above and on the earth below.
> 2:11b

Rahab put herself in the same class with everyone in the whole city of Jericho when she spoke, saying, "a great fear of you has fallen on us," and "all who live in this country are melting in fear," and "our hearts melted" and "everyone's courage failed." Everyone was terrified of a people who apparently could control water and warriors, nature and nations.

Jericho was going to fall before such an army. There was no way around it. But as we shall see, what made Rahab different from everyone else who could see the inevitability of defeat, was to *Whom* she attributed the power, the One who merited her faith.

But Rahab wasn't afraid just because of the recent military victories. She knew that they were just part of a pattern, the way this God worked.

Given the fact that prostitutes usually only ply their trade when they are young enough to be able to earn a living at it, it's not unlikely that Rahab would have been too young to have remembered the event of the crossing of the Red Sea when it happened. It may have occurred, in fact, before she was even born.

The ones who'd actually experienced it were all dead now, all two million of them, except the two, Joshua and Caleb. Those who had seen that miracle of water piling up both upstream and downstream[37] (get a hydrologist to explain how that could happen without a miracle), who had seen Pharaoh and his army with their chariot wheels falling off and then submerged by the flood that God released—all of them died with that first-hand experience still in their memories. They rejected—mistrusted, maligned—the God of that miracle.

And yet a lone prostitute forty years later was willing to trust Him. She believed.

She believed.

Chapter 4

Rahab Risks It All

Now then, please swear to me by the LORD that you will show kindness to my family, because I have shown kindness to you.

Joshua 2:12a

Hundreds of years after the time of Rahab, her most famous descendant, Jesus, would crystallize a truth in the words, "Out of the overflow of the heart the mouth speaks."[38]

With those words He showed us that the way we talk about things—how we represent people, events, feelings, and other facts—has a source. Our conversations (both with others as well as our own inner dialogues) reveal a foundation from which the words emerge. We call such a font of our words a narrative base.

A narrative base is the result of the way that you select the details of your life and give them relative importance that becomes visible in your thinking and then in your speech. For instance, a traumatic automobile accident might affect the way you think about driving a car, and thus how you would talk about driving a car. Other events of your life, such as what you wore to work last Thursday, pass out of your memory and your thinking processes because we don't consider them significant enough for that narrative base.

A believer's narrative base is one that must be consciously developed, not just allowed to "emerge." That's because there are so many competing influences in our lives that exert pressure on us to think thoughts that cause us to disregard or mistrust the Lord or His Word. For instance, if a low regard for the welfare of other human beings—a "me first attitude"—affects your thinking instead of Jesus' teaching, then your language will show that attitude. You won't put others' interests ahead of your own. Self-sacrifice will seem to you to be at best inefficient. Out of the abundance of your heart, your mouth will speak.

Rahab's words to the spies reveal clearly her narrative base: the ideas she considered important and on which she made decisions and spoke of them. Her faith, then, came out in her language. We can properly call her words "an architecture of faith," a structure that became obvious when she spoke of how she saw the power of the God of Israel. It was the basis on which she was about to take the biggest risk of her life.

She saw God's actions in protecting His people as having two qualities: They were deliberate, and they were precise.

After she'd described the God of Israel as the God of everything—both in heaven and on earth below—she must have drawn a deep breath. "Now then," she said. She was about to build on that narrative base of her knowledge of His power by asking for a favor. Quelling her own fears (and not letting them be the narrative base of her words!), she pressed her advantage, called in her markers, went for the jugular. She knew these men could help her, and she had them where she wanted them.

The first thing she did was ask for an oath in the name of this God who could send plagues, stop a river in its tracks, and feed a whole nation for 40 years. She wanted to throw in her lot with such a God. She wanted to be on the side of the ones who'd defeated her next-door-neighbor kings Sihon and Og.

She saw God's actions in protecting His people as having two qualities: They were *deliberate*, and they were *precise*. They were deliberate in the sense that she knew that the parting of the Red Sea and the defeat of their enemies weren't just coincidences. They couldn't be explained as random occurrences. She knew there was a Personality behind these events, a Power that made things happen at a certain time and in

certain way. She also saw these actions as precise in the way that they affected God's people for good and His enemies for misfortune: the waters of the Red Sea that had protected God's people from flank attacks as they walked across, were the same waters that later crashed in and drowned Pharaoh's army.

She knew that this same God could crush His enemies, and she didn't want to be His enemy. By asking for an oath in His name, she knew she put the two spies on notice that if they broke that oath, they wouldn't just have to deal with her, but Him as well, as guarantor of the oath.

Her faith in this God was the decisive element in her decision-making, the factor that trumped her uncertainties and fears. One thing was solid and dependable, and that was the nature of this God. It was a top-down universe, she would have said, one in which the invisible dimension of God would certainly have exerted irresistible power over the world she could see.

Now, we can know what Rahab believed about God by examining what she said about Him. Almost as powerful, however, is what she would have had to have rejected or excluded from her narrative base. While she accepted the power of the living God, at the same time she would have had to abandon all the false gods of her childhood, the ones her friends and perhaps even her own experience would have said had protected the impregnable city of Jericho up until that time. She would have had to reject likewise all the appearance of the military might and provisions that the city and its leaders boasted. But most important of all, she would have had to make a conscious effort to exclude from her narrative base the most powerful rival God has had throughout all history: the all-too-human tendency to fear the unknown.

Fear, she would have concluded, had no place in her narrative base if she were to follow the God who could meet all her needs as He had for the Israelites.

Rahab had only one bargaining chip: the fact that she'd saved the lives of the spies and put her own life on the line to do so. Like Abraham bargaining for Sodom[39] or Moses pleading for the lives of the rebellious people,[40] she trafficked in the only advantage she had before these men who were in her debt.

> But when God walked around on earth, very few good works or words moved Him. But faith—now, that was a different story. Faith impressed Him. It "wowed" Him.

It's true that in the Bible people have sometimes been able to persuade or dissuade God with their words. Hezekiah, for instance, when faced with news of his own impending death, reminded the Lord of his upright life and how he'd wholeheartedly served Him.[41] Infertile Hannah begged for a child, promising that when that child was born, she would give him over to the Lord's service.[42] Gideon whined until the Lord gave him three separate signs that He was serious about helping him defeat the Midianites.[43] And it worked: Hezekiah lived fifteen additional years, Hannah gave birth to Samuel, Gideon's skeptical eyes saw fire flare from a rock and a fleece that was sopping wet and then bone-dry.

But when God walked around on earth, very few good works or words moved Him. God-in-the-flesh, Jesus, was unimpressed with the legalistic perfection of the Pharisees, unpersuaded by the gymnastics of Saducean logic, and stood stone-faced before scribes who wanted to use their knowledge of the Old Testament laws to trip Him up.

But faith—now, that was a different story. Faith impressed Him. It "wowed" Him. In fact, the only time that the New Testament records that Jesus was "amazed" (the Greek word *ethaumasen*) was at the faith of the Roman centurion in Luke 7 who knew that Jesus could heal just with a word, from a distance. "I tell you," said Jesus, "I have not found such great faith even in Israel." (The only other time that Jesus was "amazed" at anything was at the lack of faith in His own hometown![44])

The exercise of faith is mankind's only hope to ever be able to "impress" God. So it was that this pitiful harlot Rahab—with no good works, no knowledge of Scripture, nothing at all to recommend herself to His notice—had at her disposal the only credentials necessary to really get God's attention: her unflinching, all-or-nothing faith in Him.

The "Sure Sign"

Give me a sure sign that you will spare the lives of my father and mother, my brothers and sisters, and all who belong to them, and that you will save us from death. 2:12b-13

In asking for a sign, Rahab unwittingly joined the ranks of many other believers in the Bible, like the aforementioned Gideon, who asked for a sign. In one case, it was a sign for guidance, as when the servant of Abraham needed some discernment in choosing a wife for Isaac.[45] In another example, Moses like Gideon had done, requested a sign that the Lord would be with him.[46] Similarly, Jonathan[47] also sought a miraculous sign before a great battle.

But what Rahab was asking was not a miraculous sign but rather a physical manifestation of the promise the spies were making to her. She wanted a pledge or a token—sort of a fact to match up with the verbal representations the spies had made with their words. She wanted something to hold onto, something visual and tactile, that would still be there when the spies were long gone.

"Our lives for your lives," the men assured her. "If you don't tell what we are doing, we will treat you kindly and faithfully when the LORD gives us the land." 2:14

How could the spies make such a promise, one they were willing to guarantee with their own lives?

The answer is easy when you look at their words, for they were speaking out of the same narrative base that Rahab had, speaking a common language. "When God gives us the land," they said, not "if God gives us the land." They knew that this battle would have only one outcome: the conquest of Jericho. They knew it so surely that they, like Rahab, were willing to stake their own existence on it. This was more than just passing gratitude for the way she'd hidden them, more than just wishful thinking and good intentions. They knew they'd have the ear of their leader Joshua and would be able to make their promise stick. But more than that, they knew that the God they served would respect—and reward—the kind of loyalty that Rahab had toward Him.

What they offered was their own deaths if hers occurred. Their lives for her life meant their death for her death. If anything went wrong during the battle, if someone slipped up and killed her even accidentally, they were willing to die.

He did it with the full knowledge that He was dying for each of us. His life for ours, He promised. Only He didn't wait for us to die to keep His promise: He died for us—in advance.

That's commitment, and we are stunned by its seriousness. But that declaration by the spies is just a pale semblance, a wispy foreshadowing of something that accompanied another announcement of a coming rescue. When Jesus faced His own imminent death, He did it with the full knowledge that He was dying for each of us. His life for ours, He promised.

Only He didn't wait for us to die to keep His promise: He died for us—in advance.

So she let them down by a rope through the window, for the house she lived in was part of the city wall. Now she had said to them, "Go to the hills so the pursuers will not find you. Hide yourselves there three days until they return, and then go on your way."

2:15-16

As the men made their preparations for a daring escape down a rope alongside the great city wall, Rahab discussed with the spies the only thing remotely resembling a timetable she would have. Three days of hiding, she thought, would be enough to let their trail get cold and increase their chances of eluding the men she knew the king would send after them.

But she wasn't willing to let them go out any exit other than her own window, the only place she knew for sure she could protect, at least for the few precious moments it would take them to scramble out into the night.

Chapter 5

The Red Cord of Hope

One of the most endearing qualities of Scripture is the way it captures human nature in just a few words. Take, for instance, the depiction of how the disciples heard Jesus' last words, found in Acts 1:4-11. Everyone wants to know a timetable, and those disciples were no different, asking Jesus just before His ascension into heaven if that were the time in which He would restore the kingdom to Israel.

The issue, He carefully explained, was not a program but a power; not an agenda but an anointing. Go wait in Jerusalem, Jesus gently advised, for a coming event unlike anything else the world had ever known.

With those words, He began to ascend into the air, and even after a cloud obscured their last glimpse of the soles of His feet, the eleven disciples still stood, openmouthed, staring at the sky.

"Men of Galilee," came a voice at their elbows. The disciples must have rubbed their aching necks as they turned to see two angels standing beside them. "Why do you stand here looking into the sky?" the heavenly beings asked. "This same Jesus, who has been taken from you into heaven, will come back in the same way you have seen him go into heaven."

Jesus' eventual return was a given, and how He'd come back—in the sky, just as He'd left—a foregone conclusion. The implication was in what the angels didn't say: "Just go and wait, as you were told." Everything was going to be all right.

Thousands of years previous, Rahab faced a similar scenario. The very window she was to use for the spies to escape would be the same window that would frame her salvation.

> The men said to her, "This oath you made us swear will not be binding on us unless, when we enter the land, you have tied this scarlet cord in the window through which you let us down . . . ."
>
> 2:17-18a

And as the disciples would discover as they waited for Jesus, only the place designated by the Lord is the right place to wait. Like the disciples, Rahab would have to do it without a timetable and no clear picture of exactly what would happen when the time did arrive.

Waiting, however, is hardly a passive activity, as anyone who's ever had to do it will affirm. For the disciples, it meant taking care of some tasks like choosing a new disciple to replace Judas and encouraging one another. But mainly it was just open-ended prayer sessions described by Luke, the author of Acts, as "constant." The idea conveyed by the Greek word here is that they just "carried on" resolutely in prayer.

Rahab was willing to follow through with the "carrying on" aspect of waiting, as her eventual rescue proves. But no one reading the words of the spies when they described the oath can come away with the impression that the whole oath and rescue arrangement was the spies' idea. Their words, "this oath *you made us swear,*" shows that the spies must have felt a little bit of compulsion in the whole arrangement—but that apparently didn't bother Rahab in the least. She knew what she wanted, and she knew they would give it to her.

We've already mentioned the example of the Canaanite woman[48] whom Jesus ignored, refused, even rebuked. She, undeterred, bantered back and forth with Him—pleading, teasing, even joking slyly—until He agreed to heal her daughter and commended her for her great faith, to boot. Another desperate woman, suffering from a hemorrhage that had made her a social outcast, literally pushed her way into Jesus' life, we read in Mark 5:24-34. Brought to the point of bankruptcy from doctor bills and in terrible pain, she elbowed her way through a crowd with the single-minded intention of just touching Jesus' cloak. Instead of being put off by her audacity, Jesus was impressed with her faith, and healed her and spoke tenderly to her.

A Pushy Kind of Faith?

Rahab was that same kind of woman, and didn't seem to mind the spies' hinting that she was a pushy woman. She was willing to put up with any condition they set, just so they agreed to come back!

We don't know where the red cord came from—perhaps the spies had it with them; or, more likely, it was made from the flax she had been drying on the roof where the spies had hidden. At any rate, it became a symbol of the oath, a representation of the words that had passed in agreement between them.

For hundreds of years believers have assumed, however, that the color of the cord was not accidental; that it was God's intention that the scarlet hue carry a kind of bonus of meaning. For the Israelites who would march around the city before climbing over its miraculously-toppled wall, the sight of a flash of red over what had been the spies' doorway of escape must have reminded them of their parents' placing of blood over their own doorways before leaving Egypt.[49] That red sign had been a signal to the Lord to pass over a house because God's people dwelt within; Rahab's red cord, similarly, meant that those within her house were under the protection of the oath of the spies.

The physical symbol must never be allowed to overshadow the meaning of what it signifies, for that is idolatry.

And from our modern-day vantage point, we Christians cannot look at a red cord and not be reminded of the way we have been marked with the *blood* of Christ, which we are told buys us back—redeems us—from all our invading enemies.[50] The ropey red substance that flowed congealing down a rough-hewn cross as it drained from His lifeless body now is

59

the daily barter for our very souls. Just as the cord of Rahab marked the exact boundaries of where the fighting and killing would stop in Jericho, so it is the blood of Christ, Colossians tells us, that calls a truce—makes peace—in each believer's life.[51]

But Rahab took very seriously the representational power of the cord that signified the oath that the men had made to her. Throughout Israelite history, many such symbols would have a powerful impact on the minds of the people. The ark, which would later precede the people in the crossing of the Jordan and then in the circling of Jericho, unfortunately became for them not just the manifestation of the presence of God among them. Many years later, it would become in their thinking like a magic charm or amulet they depended on to guarantee them success in all military engagements—a mistaken impression that God dramatically corrected when He allowed the ark to be taken in battle.[52] The message was clear: The physical symbol must never be allowed to overshadow the meaning of what it signifies, for that is idolatry.

Two Conditions

. . . and unless you have brought your father and your mother, your brothers and all your family into your house. If anyone goes outside your house into the street, his blood will be on our head if a hand is laid on him. But if you tell what we are doing, we will be released from the oath you made us swear.
"Agreed," she replied, "Let it be as you say." So she sent them away and they departed. And she tied the scarlet cord in the window.

2:18b-21

The conditions the spies put upon Rahab may seem odd at first glance. But you can see the strategic advantage of having a red cord to mark the correct household that was to be saved. Likewise, the idea of keeping all her relatives cooped up together in her house would be practical if, during the fray of battle, they were to be marked and rescued. There would be no time for going from house to house. (You could just imagine giving directions to the cousins' houses: "First you go down the first street north of the city gate . . . what? The city gate is gone? The whole wall is gone!")

Keeping all her relatives close at hand, while necessary, must have been a considerable challenge. What could have been viewed as a burden was for Rahab a manageable way of assuring herself that her loved ones were in the same safe, promise-protected place she was. It was a condition she gladly accepted.

Like all other aspects of man's dealings with God, her salvation came with conditions. While God loved mankind unconditionally enough to send His Son to die for us as a group, He nonetheless has expectations—conditions—He puts on us individually. The first condition is that we recognize some elemental truths about Him—that He is powerful, eternal, and divine. Ignore those things that even nature teaches us, Romans 1:18-20 tells us, and each of us incurs His righteous wrath, for we have no excuse for willful ignorance. He expects that such necessities as the breath of life, which He freely provides, would make us at least seek Him[53] and perhaps try to establish a relationship with Him. None of those actions would earn us such a relationship, but are simply appropriate responses to a God that would provide such a world of provision for us.

Even our salvation doesn't come without conditions. Let's leave aside all the arguments about what constitutes a "work" and what doesn't—and agree that no one is acceptable to God without acknowledging Him as Father and His Son as both Savior and Lord.

But nothing we do is commensurate with what we get. A momentary immersion in water that gets us an indwelling of the Spirit? A puny few years of life of obedience that gets us an eternity of free lunches? For Rahab, her life and those of her loved ones saved just for misdirecting some soldiers and hanging out a red cord? These aren't "fair" deals. We are the winners, every time.

And yet, they do cost us. Why, we might wonder, did Rahab have to tie the red cord out for all those days to dangle in the desert wind and cause questions from others? Couldn't the spies just have arranged a last-minute signal when she could have tossed the cord out from a hiding place? Why keep all her relatives there the whole time? Couldn't someone have sent a smoke signal that said, "One more day of circling, and then we're coming in, so gather up the in-laws?"

Faith and Hope

We may not like the truth that emerges here. God wants us to wait on His terms, not ours. Unfortunately, He's not really concerned with our convenience, but with the building of our faith.

God wants us to wait on His terms, not ours. Unfortunately, He's not really concerned with our convenience, but with the building of our faith.

Faith, Hebrews chapter 11 tells us, originates in the unseen and takes shape and form here on earth. It's the invisible quality that causes what we see to materialize. Its origin is in heaven. Words that God spoke literally became sun, moon, stars, and all of earth's features. Faith's font is the unseen—it begins there and takes substance here according to what God knows and then says.

Because faith—true faith—is based in the revealed word of God, it is the logical necessity of a believer; and Rahab was no exception. She had words, promises from God through His representatives, and those were as real to her as the cord she could touch.

However, Rahab had more than faith. She had another element, faith's counterpart, which is *hope*. While faith has a directional nature—originating in the words and will of God and taking shape here on earth—hope has another direction. It does indeed share the unseen character of faith (hope that is seen is no hope at all, Scripture tells us[54]) but its direction of travel is different.

Hope depends upon the "unchangeable things in which it is impossible for God to lie," Hebrews 6:18 tells us. That hope becomes something we can hold onto, encouragement from God Himself, "an anchor for the soul, firm and secure."[55] In one sense, then, hope is a static, stabilizing factor. But hope is also active, going before us into the innermost reaches of heaven itself. Unlike faith whose mooring point is in heaven, hope travels back.

"It enters the inner sanctuary behind the curtain," the writer of Hebrews continues, "where Jesus, who went before us, has entered on our behalf." Like the persistent widow who just kept coming back, upstart hope never tires in its daily, hourly, sometimes moment-to-moment entrance beyond the veil to present its own substance, its own requests there.

Rahab had every reason for hope. It was by faith that she was able to preserve her own life and those of the people she loved. But it was by hope that she was able to keep herself sane in the process.

Rahab had every reason for hope. It was by faith that she was able to preserve her own life and those of the people she loved. But it was by hope that she was able to keep herself sane in the process. It was by that act of the will, exercising the pro-active part of faith, because faith is the ability to be certain of what we hope for.[56]

Rahab had every reason for hope, every reason for her mind to continually go behind the veil of the presence of God. Her hope was based on faith in the character of the One who ultimately backed up the promises the spies made to her.

The promises, after all, were only as good as the integrity of the Promiser, and only as dependable as His ability to keep them.

Chapter 6

The Inevitability of Fulfillment of the Promise

 When they left, they went into the hills and stayed there three days until the pursuers had searched all along the road and returned without finding them. Then the two men started back. They went down out of the hills, forded the river and came to Joshua son of Nun and told him everything that had happened to them. They said to Joshua, "The LORD has surely given the whole land into our hands; all the people are melting in fear because of us."

                                                          Joshua 2:22-24

Forty years before the spies had come to Jericho, Moses had stopped at the edge of the Red Sea and surveyed the armies of Pharaoh—corpses that lay washed up on the distant shore of the Red Sea. Moses had begun to sing, and in that song he described the Lord who had accomplished this victory as "a warrior."

People would talk about this event for the rest of the history of the world. For nations that would oppose that Warrior, Moses concluded, the story would be one that would fill them with fear. The people of Canaan, in particular, would "melt away" as "terror and dread would fall upon them."[57]

Imagine how those spies, four decades after Moses sang his victory song, must have reacted when they heard a Canaanite woman describing her city as "melting in fear." Surely the prophecy of Moses was fulfilled.

⌒⌒⌒

The battle was already won, simply because the Lord said it would be.

And so it was when the spies escaped from their three-day hideout in the mountains, they went directly to Joshua to report the condition of the land they were about to invade. We are not told in Scripture what they thought of Rahab. But one thing is unmistakable: they used the exact words of this lowly prostitute—and only her words—in their report. The people were melting in fear, and the Lord would surely give the land into the hands of the Israelites.

That was it. No reports on strategic defenses of the city, no assessment of armies nor armaments. No ambush plans, no weak spots in perimeters, not even a spy inside the city to open gates nor an underground movement to aid from within. The battle was already won, simply because the Lord said it would be.

The inhabitants of Jericho had been living a lie for generations, believing that they owned the city or the land around it. No matter how far back in history a Jerichoite or other Canaanite could trace ownership of land and property, no matter how many deeds and bills of sale and surveys they owned, no matter how many ancient boundary stones marked inheritances, no matter now many writs in the city courthouse of Jericho stood inscribed on stacked clay tablets, they were all just illusions. They may have received money for lands, rented it out, and willed it to heirs—but it never belonged to them.

For the four hundred years the Israelites had been away from the land, and for the preceding years when Joseph and Jacob and Isaac had walked throughout that promised land, and even during the lifetime of Abraham who never had a written deed, that land belonged to God's people, no matter what interlopers happened to be squatting on it and selling it to each other. It never belonged to them, because God who owned it had deeded it to His people, and to them alone.

Not only were the people and their claim to the land not a threat to the Israelites, they were actually an advantage to them. As Moses had told God's people for years, those who crossed the Jordan to conquer the land would one day be living in houses built by others, drinking water from wells others dug, eating produce from fields and vineyards planted by others, herding animals they'd neither bought nor bred. Numbers 14:9, which records the words of Joshua and Caleb describing the inhabitants of the land, says in the NIV, "we will swallow them up"; but actually it could be more accurately translated from the Hebrew as, "those people shall become food for you."[58]

The spies in reporting back to Joshua saw no obstacles to the taking of the city, indeed in taking the whole land. The militaristic ability of the Israelites simply was not a factor. They had come to the same conclusion that Jonathan would voice many years later, "Nothing can hinder the LORD from saving, whether by many or by few."[59]

They believed in the inevitability of success not *just* because Jericho was melting away psychologically. They weren't going to take that enormous powerful fortified metropolis just because of mind games. They were going to take it because the Lord had given it to them, and because He'd said it, it would come true.

Facts and Representations

Remember in a previous lesson we discussed how the facts of our past are inaccessible to us, except through representations? We spoke about how it is for us humans that we see an event, or touch an object, and it is converted into representations in our heads. In that sense, for humans, facts precede and form representations.

In another sense, sometimes representations precede facts. Take the example of an artist. That artist will have in her head a representation of a painting that she's going to create. From that mental picture, she will put paint on canvas and make that representation she's had in her head into a fact of a painting.

That limited ability that we as humans have to represent objects before they actually exist is an ability that God has without limits. In fact, it is the way in which He created everything in existence. His first action of creation was to speak—

represent linguistically—a concept that would become fact, the speaking-forth-creation of light. When we say He spoke everything else into existence, we are saying that His representations became facts by virtue of His powerful ability to do so.

When the Israelites were out in the desert, God instructed them carefully on the pros and cons of His ability to make His representations into facts in their lives. Obey Me, He said, and I'll make every aspect of this land cooperate to make you rich—rain, agricultural abundance, lots of children—and every enemy you have will be conquered so you can live in complete peace of mind.[60] But if you decide to be pig-headed and do things your way and ignore Me, I'll use my powers to make My representations into facts you won't like at all: you'll fail financially, politically, and in both physical and mental health.[61]

Not only can He and does He use His power to represent coming facts, He is also gracious enough to let us in on what He's doing before He acts. "See, the former things have taken place," He says in Isaiah 42:9, "and new things I declare; before they spring into being I announce them to you." The same thought is echoed in Romans 4:17, which speaks of "the God who gives life to the dead and calls things that are not as though they were."

There's another, compelling way that Scripture shows us that God's representations precede and form facts. Think about this. Though Jesus Christ has certainly existed as a fact from all eternity, even Jesus was portrayed as a representation that became a fact on the earth—He literally was the *Word that became flesh.*[62]

The question, of course, is not whether or not God has the power to represent coming events and then make them happen. The question for us is whether or not we will accept His representations over what we think.

Eve found this out. In the garden of Eden, she and her husband Adam were told they could eat from any tree they chose except for the tree of the knowledge of good and evil. "If you do that," God warned them, "you'll die." It could be argued that since Eve and Adam were the first humans and no death had occurred on the earth, they hadn't experienced death and therefore didn't know what it was. But they had experienced God's representations of a coming event! He said, "You'll die."

With the issue of death, the same is true for each of us. Though we may contend that we have *witnessed* the death of others, none of us can say that we have death in our own personal experience. We just know the representations of it, and there's only One who knows about it from firsthand experience and has come back to share what's ahead. All that God tells us comes out of His vast representational storehouse of knowledge of the future.

Any of our representations are only of the past, because for us, the future doesn't exist! The only way we can represent the future is by accepting what God says about it, because what He represents about it will inevitably come true.

That's what the spies were saying when they used Rahab's words. God's promises—verbal representations—that He would give them the land were about to become cold hard facts of reality.

Rahab Goes into Hiding

From this point on in Rahab's story, we do not know what she said or what she thought. She had told the spies to go into hiding for three days, so we can assume she didn't think during those three days that they'd be back. We can assume she spent at least part of that time buying food and other provisions for what might be an extended time. During this time as well, she must somehow have convinced her extended family to come to her house. "For how long?" they must have asked.

> *She did this with her eyes wide open: she knew that God would save someone who trusted Him and was obedient to Him.*

But in reality, Rahab had no deadline past the three days. Faith, for her, meant an open-ended schedule of trust.

She did this with her eyes wide open: she knew that God would save someone who trusted Him and was obedient to Him. But she knew *this* God's power could be turned against someone as well as toward them for their help and protection. This God would put those who accused Him of being powerless and vindictive—those who'd said He'd led them out to the desert to kill them—this same God could put the faithless and ungrateful to death. It was with this God that Rahab threw in her lot.

Rahab had submitted to a batch of representations in the form of a promise. She had put all her eggs in one basket. There were no contingency plans for a woman who "knew" the Lord had given the land to the invading army.

Her "action options" to stay alive had narrowed down to a list of one:

Wait.

Chapter 7

The Lesson of the Stones

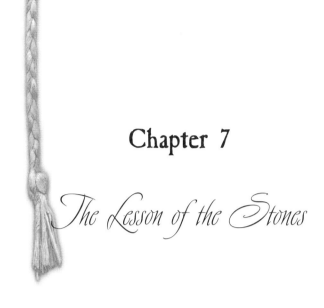

Joshua 3:1–4:24

Early in the morning Joshua and all the Israelites set out from Shittim and went to the Jordan, where they camped before crossing over. After three days the officers went throughout the camp, giving orders to the people: "When you see the ark of the covenant of the LORD your God, and the priests, who are Levites, carrying it, you are to move out from your positions and follow it. Then you will know which way to go, since you have never been this way before. But keep a distance of about a thousand yards between you and the ark; do not go near it."

Joshua told the people, "Consecrate yourselves, for tomorrow the LORD will do amazing things among you."

Joshua said to the priests, "Take up the ark of the covenant and pass on ahead of the people." So they took it up and went ahead of them.

And the LORD said to Joshua, "Today I will begin to exalt you in the eyes of all Israel, so they may know that I am with you as I was with Moses. Tell the priests who carry the ark of the covenant: 'When you reach the edge of the Jordan's waters, go and stand in the river.'"

Joshua said to the Israelites, "Come here and listen to the words of the LORD your God. This is how you will know that the living God is among you and that he will certainly drive out before you the Canaanites, Hittites, Hivites, Perizzites, Girgashites, Amorites and Jebusites. See, the ark of the covenant of the LORD of all the earth will go into the Jordan ahead of you. "Now then, choose twelve men from the tribes of Israel, one from each tribe. And as soon as the priests who carry the ark of the LORD—the LORD of all the earth—set foot in the Jordan, its waters flowing downstream will be cut off and stand up in a heap."

So when the people broke camp to cross the Jordan, the priests carrying the ark of the covenant went ahead of them. Now the Jordan is at flood stage all during harvest. Yet as soon as the priests who carried the ark reached the Jordan and their feet touched the water's edge, the water from upstream stopped flowing. It piled up in a heap a great distance away, at a town called Adam in the vicinity of Zarethan, while the water flowing down to the Sea of the Arabah (the Salt Sea) was completely cut off. So the people crossed over opposite Jericho. The priests who carried the ark of the covenant of the LORD stood firm on dry ground in the middle of the Jordan, while all Israel passed by until the whole nation had completed the crossing on dry ground.

When the whole nation had finished crossing the Jordan, the LORD said to Joshua, "Choose twelve men from among the people, one from each tribe, and tell them to take up twelve stones from the middle of the Jordan from right where the priests stood and to carry them over with you and put them down at the place where you stay tonight."

So Joshua called together the twelve men he had appointed from the Israelites, one from each tribe, and said to them, "Go over before the ark of the LORD your God into the middle of the Jordan. Each of you is to take up a stone on his shoulder, according to the number of the tribes of the Israelites, to serve as a sign among you. In the future, when your children ask you, 'What do these stones mean?' tell them that the flow of the Jordan was cut off before the ark of the covenant of the LORD. When it crossed the Jordan, the waters of the Jordan were cut off. These stones are to be a memorial to the people of Israel forever."

So the Israelites did as Joshua commanded them. They took twelve stones from the middle of the Jordan, according to the number of the tribes of the Israelites, as the LORD had told Joshua; and they carried them over with them to their camp, where they put them down. Joshua set up the twelve stones that had been in the middle of the Jordan at the spot where the priests who carried the ark of the covenant had stood. And they are there to this day.

Now the priests who carried the ark remained standing in the middle of the Jordan until everything the LORD had commanded Joshua was done by the people, just as Moses had directed Joshua. The people hurried over, and as soon as all of them had crossed, the ark of the LORD and the priests came to the other side while the people watched. The men of Reuben, Gad and the half-tribe of Manasseh crossed over, armed, in front of the Israelites, as Moses had directed them. About forty thousand armed for battle crossed over before the LORD to the plains of Jericho for war.

That day the LORD exalted Joshua in the sight of all Israel; and they revered him all the days of his life, just as they had revered Moses.

Then the LORD said to Joshua, "Command the priests carrying the ark of the Testimony to come up out of the Jordan."

So Joshua commanded the priests, "Come up out of the Jordan."

And the priests came up out of the river carrying the ark of the covenant of the LORD. No sooner had they set their feet on the dry ground than the waters of the Jordan returned to their place and ran at flood stage as before.

On the tenth day of the first month the people went up from the Jordan and camped at Gilgal on the eastern border of Jericho. And Joshua set up at Gilgal the twelve stones they had taken out of the Jordan. He said to the Israelites, "In the future when your descendants ask their fathers, 'What do these stones mean?' tell them, 'Israel crossed the Jordan on dry ground.' For the LORD your God dried up the Jordan before you until you had crossed over. The LORD your God did to the Jordan just what he had done to the Red Sea when he dried it up before us

73

until we had crossed over. He did this so that all the peoples of the earth might know that the hand of the LORD is powerful and so that you might always fear the LORD your God."

As Rahab waited, something extraordinary was going on at the banks of the nearby Jordan River. A massive force of more than two million people—men, women, children—had assembled at the far side of the river and had camped there.

They were as much in the dark about upcoming events as was Rahab. Though she remained ensconced in Jericho, it is unlikely that she would have been completely ignorant of events in the Israelite camp after the spies left her. There are two reasons to suppose she would have known some things. First, her home was on the city wall, with a window to the outside. It is not impossible that her window faced the Jordan River that would be the arena of coming action. Secondly, spying was not exclusively an Israelite activity; and what Rahab didn't see herself must have been reported by the king's own spies and lookouts. After all, it's pretty difficult to move two million people around without somebody noticing!

At the point that the Israelites begin to cross the Jordan, the spies have been gone from Rahab for six days. For the Israelites, life as they'd always known it was about to change. For forty years, regular as clockwork, there had been some never-varying daily events: the falling of manna during every night except the Sabbath, shoes that never wore out, and funerals. There was never a tent that escaped tears.[63] The sound of mourning for parents never left the camp, for the people who'd seen the Ten Plagues and the piling up of waters upstream and downstream of the Red Sea had accused both God and Moses of not caring about them and their children. Those same children, helpless and dependent, learned the hard lesson that we should put our trust in the character of a God who can—and will—perform miracles to protect His people.

Thus it was that a new generation, most of whom had been too young to remember the Red Sea, camped there a few miles from Jericho on the banks of the river where, hundreds of years later, the Savior of the world would be baptized. We don't usually think of God as putting on repeat performances of miracles, but He was about to become the God of encores as He repeated for this new generation the same miracle He'd done for their fathers and mothers. Acting on God's instructions, Joshua told the priests to go out to the edge of the Jordan River, and carrying the ark of the covenant, to stand in the river. Even though it was at flood stage, the water immediately stopped flowing and piled up in a heap some twenty miles upstream at a town called Adam.

Twelve men, representing the tribes of Israel, each took a big rock from the middle of the riverbed after the people had crossed over. Those rocks were put in a big pile where the people camped that night after crossing the river, to serve the purpose God had told Joshua: as a "sign" of what had happened. Never again would God repeat the miracle of stopping a river for an entire nation.

Facts and Representations

What had happened at that river was a fact. It happened at a certain time on a certain spring day about 1400 BC. At the moment the last people to cross it wiped the sand from their sandal soles, the event closed, so to speak. From that point on, the people were to look to the pile of stones to remember the event.

When children who would later be born would ask their parents, "What do those stones mean?" the parents were to tell them that the stones were a *representation* of that past *fact*. Nobody could get back into the Jordan River to experience what had happened to them, but the parents could point to the stones and tell their children that rocks which had been in the middle of a raging, flood-swollen river were suddenly left high and dry just where they stood. And this was because of the power of a God who had outlived their parents and would outlive them, a God of Red Sea miracles and Jordan River miracles and all future miracles. This kind of powerful God, the parents would tell their children, was Someone that everybody should respect and obey.

People of all cultures and all times have used this type of

representation to remind them of past events. A wedding ring recalls a ceremony and vows made. A cornerstone marker commemorates the beginning of building an edifice, and a tombstone the end of a life.

And yet we recognize when we look at the ring or the cornerstone marker or the tombstone that those are not the events. The events are facts. The symbols of them are representations, but they are not the facts themselves. A father telling his son about the crossing of the Jordan would know instinctively, as would his son, that the stones symbolize the event which was a fact that cannot be experienced in any way except through a representation of it.

We call those kinds of representations that are accessed through our senses *iconic representations*. They are symbols of a physical nature of something. Like the *icons* on a computer screen, they are not the facts themselves but a way of accessing the facts.

The same is true of any physical experience we have. When we look at a mountain, our brains form an *icon* inside our heads. We know that's true—the whole mountain isn't inside our heads, is it? And we turn away from the mountain or even travel thousands of miles from it, we still have an *icon* of it in our heads that we remember.

When we touch and then savor the coolness of an iced beverage, what we have in our brains is an *icon* of that coolness and flavor. We remember its refreshing, tingling taste through an *icon* in our brain—for the glass and its contents stay on the table for but a few minutes but can remain as icons in our memories for years. Scientists tell us that the most powerful *icon*-marker of all our senses is the sense of smell. Ever passed a stranger in a supermarket that's wearing cologne that transports you back to your high school prom?

But let's return to the father years ago who tells his son about the pile of rocks from the Jordan River. It's true that in those rocks they had an iconic, or visual, symbol of that past event. My friend, Marq Toombs, recently took his family on a vacation, and his children had gathered pretty rocks from their grandmother's backyard. Weeks after they returned home, they would bring out the rocks and recall a special event or fond memory from that time at her house. By talking about it, they were representing the vacation in yet another way—*linguistically*. They used words to evoke the same memories in others in the family, and to share stories about the vacation.

The Hebrew father who showed his son the Jordan rocks would be showing him an iconic representation of that past event. But he also represented it with language, too, saying, "Israel crossed the Jordan on dry ground. For the LORD your God dried up the Jordan before you until you had crossed over. The LORD your God did to the Jordan just what he had done to the Red Sea when he dried it up before us until we had crossed over. He did this so that the peoples of the earth might know that the hand of the LORD is powerful, and so that you might always fear the LORD your God."[64]

We act on our fears and our pride instead of the Word of God that promises us peace and help if we will do things His way and not our own.

Now, which of the representations—the *iconic* (the rocks) or the explanation of how they got there (linguistic) would be the most useful to the little boy in understanding the meaning of the rocks? Though the stacked stones would be impressive, they would not accurately and completely represent the crossing of the Jordan and all it meant without the words that told how the rocks got to where they now reposed.

Though those rocks stood for many years in the same place, they are no longer in place. We do not know the date or the circumstances in which they were scattered or carried off, but no archaeologist has, to date, found them. Yet the linguistic representation of the crossing of the Jordan is still with us—in the book of Joshua.

Iconic representations—those ways we use sight, touch, hearing, smelling, and tasting to represent facts—have limited usefulness. Sight, for instance, keeps us from walking into walls, but from God's point of view, icons are always partial, for they can't tell us the whole truth about anything! Yet how often we use our bodily senses to make decisions! Esau was hungry, and because of that powerful iconic representation of the ache in his belly, he sold his birthright to his brother in exchange for a meal. The ten spies who went with Joshua and Caleb on a reconnaissance trip into Canaan all saw the same giants and fortified walls. They were facts. Yet when they returned, the ten spies linguistically represented the walls as too high, the cities too powerful, the giant inhabitants too daunting.[65] In spite of the verbal representation of God through Moses that the Lord would do all the fighting and that they didn't have to be afraid, the ten spies persuaded everyone but Joshua and Caleb and Moses that what their eyes had seen had told them the truth about the situation. They chose their iconic representations over the linguistic representations of God.[66]

How many times we do the same. We crave a certain food and eat way past satisfying our hunger, in spite of what the Bible says about gluttony. We feel a tickle of attraction toward a married man and go ahead and flirt. We are afraid of the stares when we arrive late so we break speed laws. We act on our fears and our pride instead of the Word of God that promises us peace and help if we will do things His way and not our own.

All experiences in our lives are converted into representations; and how we deal with those representations will mark us as faithful or faithless.

Thus the question could legitimately be asked: Why was Rahab saved while hundreds of thousands of Jews died in the desert?

Representations, my dear, representations.

Chapter 8

Circumcision and Passover

While Rahab waits in her home in Jericho, God is active. While she must daily enforce a lack of action on her own consciousness and behavior and those of her other family members—a strategy of doing nothing overt[67]—God is in the business of creating symbols, orchestrating two events that will endure as representations that will shape the consciousness of His people forever. In a way, these two events—the practice of circumcision and the annual eating of the Passover dinner—are not new, because He had instituted both years before. Circumcision was part of God's 400-year-old covenant with Abraham and all his descendants, and the first Passover was celebrated forty years ago when Moses led the people out of Egypt.

But in another aspect, these things were new to Joshua's people. All the circumcised men, their fathers, uncles, and grandfathers now lay dead, buried in Sinai's sands. And likewise few, if any, had ever eaten the Passover dinner God had commanded be eaten yearly.

A lot of rituals and practices throughout Jewish history would become very important to them. Styles of dress, with phylacteries and prayer shawls, would mark them as distinctive at certain periods of time. Temple worship, with all the details of blood sacrifices and specific offerings, would dominate their daily life for centuries. But the styles of dress would change, and the Temple be razed to the ground.

But even now, thousands of years later, Jews still circumcise their little boys, and eat the Passover supper with their families. In a sense, God held up a military campaign for nearly a week to emphasize the importance of these two symbols that endure even to the twenty-first century.

Circumcision

Joshua 5:1-9

Now when all the Amorite kings west of the Jordan and all the Canaanite kings along the coast heard how the LORD had dried up the Jordan before the Israelites until we had crossed over, their hearts melted and they no longer had the courage to face the Israelites.

At that time the LORD said to Joshua, "Make flint knives and circumcise the Israelites again." So Joshua made flint knives and circumcised the Israelites at Gibeath Haaraloth.

Now this is why he did so: All those who came out of Egypt—all the men of military age—died in the desert on the way after leaving Egypt. All the people that came out had been circumcised, but all the people born in the desert during the journey from Egypt had not. The Israelites had moved about in the desert forty years until all the men who were of military age when they left Egypt had died, since they had not obeyed the LORD. For the LORD had sworn to them that they would not see the land that he had solemnly promised their fathers to give us, a land flowing with milk and honey. So he raised up their sons in their place, and these were the ones Joshua circumcised. They were still uncircumcised because they had not been circumcised on the way. And after the whole nation had been circumcised, they remained where they were in camp until they were healed.

Then the LORD said to Joshua, "Today I have rolled away the reproach of Egypt from you." So the place has been called Gilgal to this day.

The miracle of the crossing of the Jordan River had a profound psychological effect on all the rulers and people surrounding that geographical area. Though the Israelites had not launched a single military strike other than the battles against Sihon and Og, the actions of the Israelites' sponsoring God unnerved the heavily armed and well-trained nations that heard of it. Traditional military wisdom would have dictated that the Israelites press their advantage against the emotional weakness of their enemies. Instead, their God has them do something that will make the Israelite fighting men physically weak and unable to defend themselves.[68]

It would have taken the Israelites several days to recover from the painful process of having each man's foreskin cut away with a flint knife. But this was not commanded by God just to give the men a chance to think about their own weakness versus the power of God (though it certainly must have had that effect!). Instead, it had a much deeper meaning.

Thus a circumcision functioned as witness of compliance with that covenant, and like a wedding ring or bill of sale, it served as an iconic representation of that agreement.

When God first commanded that Abraham circumcise all the males in his household some 450 years earlier, He had done so to seal a covenant between Himself and all of Abraham's descendants. This covenant had several promises attached to it, among them that God would bless all nations through Abraham, and that He would give the land of Canaan to those descendants. Thus a circumcision functioned as witness of compliance with that covenant; and like a wedding ring or bill of sale, it served as an iconic representation of that agreement.

In time, the presence of a man's foreskin would come to signify an out-of-covenant status: unclean, disobedient, not included in the promises. Cutting away the foreskin came to mean more than just a ceremony, it was a durable symbol, one that by its irreversible nature came to signify a kind of commitment that you can't back out of.

All these things were present in the act of circumcision that day in Gilgal when the reproachful behavior of their fathers was rolled away into oblivion.

But even more, the act of circumcision carved into the flesh of those men the deed to the land they'd been promised, a land now within their sight.

The Passover

On the evening of the fourteenth day of the month, while camped at Gilgal on the plains of Jericho, the Israelites celebrated the Passover. The day after the Passover, that very day, they ate some of the produce of the land: unleavened bread and roasted grain. The manna stopped the day after they ate this food from the land; there was no longer any manna for the Israelites, but that year they ate of the produce of Canaan.

5:10-12

There must have been an air of jarring unreality on this day of great transitions. Children who had been raised from childhood with the wafers-and-honey taste of manna for breakfast, lunch, and dinner were going to come of age in God's sight by eating an extraordinary meal. The Passover—a meal of unleavened bread, roasted lamb, and other symbolic foods—represented the haste in which their fathers and mothers had left Egypt. It was a meal of fellowship with the God Who'd rescued them, and fellowship as well with the people who'd first eaten such a meal forty years before in Egypt, and only one other time in the desert a little over a year later (Numbers 9:1-6).

Deuteronomy chapter 6 shows us this remarkable aspect of this dinner. Not only were the people to reproduce the iconic symbols God had prescribed for them this special night each year, they were to use those symbols to link themselves to the people who'd first celebrated it. "In the future, when your son asks you, 'What is the meaning of the stipulations, decrees and laws the LORD our God has commanded you?'" Moses advised his people, "tell him, 'We were slaves of Pharaoh in Egypt . . .'" (Deuteronomy 6:20-21). Now what is so remarkable about a father telling his son such a thing is that nobody saying those words (except Joshua and Caleb) had actually *been* slaves in Egypt.

Yet they were to appropriate that history, those representations, as if they had happened to them personally. To this very day, when a Jewish family sits down at Passover dinner, the father recites the *Haggadah*, a standardized text for the ceremony. In it he says, *"Avadim hayinu l'Pharaoh b'Mitzrayim"*—"We were slaves of Pharaoh in Egypt." Then later, the father tells his children about "what the LORD did for me when I left Egypt."

The Passover, thus, is an example of how God's representations of a history can be—and should be— impressed on our psychology.

Thus the story of the Exodus is his own story, as if he'd experienced the events himself. Since all experience is converted into representations—memories, words, books, photographs, and other types of representations—the father tells his children that he accepts the Biblical representations, the story, as if he'd personally experienced it.

The Passover, thus, is an example of how God's representations of a history can be—and should be—impressed on our psychology. How greatly this contrasts with how we usually look at what we call "history," which is the way that the psychology of an individual or individuals is impressed upon a record of events.

What Is Reliable History?

It's no wonder that the Bible calls our present troubles "light and momentary,"[69] because all the facts of our life are moment by moment passing into the past, and are only accessible through representations: either physical symbols or our own memories.

We've already shown that you can't go back to any past event—whether it is something that happened in your childhood or five minutes ago. In fact, when you opened this book and began to read it, your impressions of it were formed as representations in your mind. You can't repeat anything—even if you open the book and begin anew to read it, you will be a different person who has already been affected by something you read the first time—even if you didn't understand it, that memory-representation will affect the next reading.

The world regards historical accounts, especially those based on first-person witness accounts, as being the most reliable. However, human history is incomplete and faulty because humans with incomplete and faulty representational abilities write it. When you read the historical account of an event, you are really reading the psychology of the writer—what he thought was important. Even if you read the compilation of multiple experts on an event, you are still dealing with a collectivity of faulty and incomplete abilities to represent; and the finished product reflects this.

Thus we can begin to appreciate the immense value of the Bible: a complete and accurate accounting of the mind of God and its interworkings with the minds of men.

A very timely example of the way that "history" reflects the psychology of the writer of the history is illustrated by the recent tendency to "revise" history books for the public schools. The sensitivities of our generation are written back into the events of the past—a process that hardly adds more accuracy, just more acceptability to the current reader.

But the people who witness events can't be relied upon to be complete and accurate from an eternal point of view, for each works from within the framework of his own proclivities and interests: his own psychology. What a witness will remember and relate are those details he or she thinks are memorable or significant. Thus any witness is limited by individual attention to detail, and limited even more just by inability to be everywhere and see everything. Even an eyewitness to a pivotal battle, for instance, can only see part of the action; and cannot correctly assess the importance of actions whose fruition may not appear for a generation or two. The same would be true even of a group of eyewitnesses: just because they agreed on the details of a situation, or even add supplemental details, would not necessarily mean that they could assess what was truly important.

Thus we can begin to appreciate the immense value of the Bible: a complete and accurate accounting of the mind of God and its interworkings with the minds of men. Because the Bible is inspired by God Himself, it is the only reliable source of information about how to live life. Though individual writers such as the physician Luke or the former tax collector Matthew may occasionally show us some glimpse of their personal interests; nonetheless the ironclad grip of the Holy Spirit on their minds as they wrote made sure that everything they wrote was not only accurate in conveying what happened, but more important, accurate in what was important about the events of which they wrote. Thus the Bible reflects a mind's psychology as well: the psychology, if you will, of the Holy Spirit of God.

Rahab's Adoption

A few meters away from the shores of the Jordan where drops of dried blood from the mass circumcision laying in the dirt, and where the scraps from the Passover meal were thrown out, Rahab stood waiting in her home. Perhaps she could even see the movements of people as the men stood in line to submit to the flint knife of Joshua; perhaps she witnessed the roasting of thousands of lambs over open pits.

Only later, after she'd been rescued from the crumbling city of Jericho, would she have verbal representations given to her to clarify what happened there, the explanations of the icons of surgeries and seders.

But something even more meaningful would happen one year from that date, when Rahab, now a part of the Israelite nation, would herself sit down to a meal of lamb and unleavened bread. Then she, like the hundreds of thousands of Israelites with whom she'd cast her lot, would speak in the first person of an event forty-one years before, as if she'd been there.

Across history, we can almost hear the voice of Rahab, as she, too, whispered:

"I was a slave in Egypt . . . ."

Chapter 9

The Ancient Voice of Jesus

 We usually think of the words of Jesus as found only in the New Testament, particularly in the books of Matthew, Mark, Luke, and John. In addition, we have recorded in the book of Acts His words to Saul on the road to Damascus and other revelations to Paul; the account of Jesus' statements at the Last Supper as revealed also to Paul; and of course His words to John in the book of Revelation.

But our heritage of His words is much, much richer than just what we find in the New Testament. That's because of the instances in which He communicated with people long before His birth in Bethlehem. Each of these remarkable events is referred to by Bible scholars as a *theophany* (from the Greek words for God and revealing), or more specifically as a *Christophany* (from the words for Christ and revealing).

Usually, a theophany in the Bible is one in which God takes human form. However, there are some notable exceptions. For instance, the Holy Spirit appeared in the form of a dove at the baptism of Jesus. Earlier in human history, God appeared to Moses in a burning bush,[70] to Abraham as a smoking fire pot with a blazing torch[71] and to the Israelites in the desert as a cloud by day and a pillar of fire by night.[72]

Most generally, though, an Old Testament theophany, or pre-mortal appearance of Jesus, involves a figure in human form who appears to a "regular person," bringing supernatural information. The physical appearance of such a messenger is usually not extraordinary, though often the being is called an angel (which is perfectly appropriate, since both the Greek and Hebrew words for "angel" carry the idea of someone who is sent or deputized to perform a task; as well as the more common meaning of an angel in the more traditional sense).[73]

The Angel of the Lord

There's a very specialized usage of the term, "the Angel of the Lord," in the Old Testament for many of these pre-mortal appearances of Jesus. Since the Bible repeatedly assures us that no one has seen the Father at any time, we can assume that any appearance of a Being who accepts worship and speaks as God would have to be Jesus. (This is in great contrast to an "ordinary" angel, who would *not* accept the worship of humans. For instance, in Revelation 22:1-9, John wanted to worship the angel who brought him his visions of the river of life and other wonders. But when John fell down to worship this "regular" angel, he rebuked him, saying, "Do not do it! I am a fellow servant with you and with your brothers the prophets and all who keep the words of this book. Worship God!"—verse 9).

The theophanies of Jesus as the *Angel of the Lord* are fascinating and varied. Please note that these are like "guest appearances," or temporary manifestations that occurred at different times long before Jesus took on a human body for some 33 years.

Here are a few of those Old Testament theophanies:

- In both Genesis 16 and 21, the young slave woman Hagar encountered the *Angel of the Lord,* someone she identified both as Lord and as God (Genesis 16:13).

- The patriarch Jacob received instructions from an Angel in Genesis 31:10-13 and later in Genesis 32 wrestled with a being he identified as both man and God (verses 22-31)[76].

- The *Angel of the Lord* in Numbers 22 prevented the northern Mesopotamian soothsayer Balaam from reckless action that would have harmed God's people (verse 32).

- The *Angel of the Lord* identified Himself as the one who brought the Israelites out of Egypt in Judges 2:1-5.

- Gideon, in Judges chapter 6, encounters a Being that is both identified as an *Angel* and as the Lord. In this remarkable account, we see Jesus sitting serenely under an oak tree, watching Gideon as he prepares a sacrifice to Him.

- Manoah and his wife, parents of Samson, saw the *Angel of the Lord* and concluded that they had seen God and yet not died (Judges chapter 13). Here, too, we see the pre-mortal Jesus waiting patiently for the couple as they killed a young goat to sacrifice to Him.

- King David saw an *Angel* who "stood between heaven and earth, with a drawn sword in his hand, extended over Jerusalem." In this unusual episode, found in 1 Chronicles 21, we see the pre-mortal Jesus involved in the carrying out of a judgment for sin, just as He will do at the end of time.[77]

- The *Angel of the Lord* has a dialogue with the Lord God (the Father) and with another angel and the prophet Zechariah, resulting in a remarkable situation where the Father spoke to an agitated angel to comfort him (Zechariah 1:1-13).

There are other instances of the actions of the *Angel of the Lord* in the Old Testament, but I have saved the two most significant ones for last: that of Abraham, and that of Joshua outside the walls of Jericho.

In the life of Abraham, we see many elements that show the richness and variety of the ways that the Bible refers to the theophany he saw.

Three beings appeared to Abraham in Genesis chapter 18. We learn in the first verse that "the LORD" appeared to Abraham, but as the story unfolds in verse 2, there are three "men" who come to him. But by verse 10, it is "the LORD" who tells Abraham about the upcoming birth of his son Isaac, and two "angels" (Genesis 19:1) who go on to Sodom to rescue Lot. So in this single incident, we see how the same pre-mortal Jesus could be referred to as a man (the way He looked to Abraham), as the *Angel of the Lord* (His function as a messenger to Abraham) and as the Lord (Himself God, with the right to command Abraham and Sarah and also the ability to bring about a miraculous birth of their son Isaac the coming year).

Abraham's life showed the involvement of the *Angel of the Lord* in the phases of faith: the promise (as we just saw in Genesis 18) and also in the contradiction phase of faith, when Abraham had to reason his way to obey the command of God to kill Isaac, the son of promise through whom all the world would be blessed. It was the *Angel of the Lord* who ended this stage of contradiction when He commanded Abraham to not kill the child. (How touching it is to realize that Jesus, as the *Angel of the Lord*, was able to stop the sacrifice of a son of promise; while there would be no one to stop the sacrifice of Himself, the ultimate Son, the fulfillment of all promises, on the cross.)

The Pan-Temporal Jesus

What all these instances of the activity of Jesus as the *Angel of the Lord* show us is that He has been intimately involved with God's people from the beginning of time, and not just during the three decades He lived in a human body here upon earth. He didn't just pop in and out of human history. He's been here with us, struggling with His people, all along.

From the instances that are listed above, we have seen Him as fearless leader, patient with the apprehensions and requests of people, nonplussed as He answers the same questions over and over. He kept people from reckless actions and corrected their misconceptions; but also was willing to wait around for people anxious to honor Him by cooking Him meals and offering other sacrifices, just because they wanted to show Him love and respect.

As the greatest pan-temporal—across all time—sacrifice, Jesus was the lamb that was slain, from the creation of the world.[78] In His role as the *Angel of the Lord*, He proved Himself long before His birth, long before His death on the cross: He didn't wait to come to earth in a body before showing His concern and love for the human race, and most overtly His protective love for those who are completely committed to Him.

In fact, what we see in the theophanies are pictures of *a God who literally just couldn't wait to come and help His people.* With that in mind, it seems natural that He would be waiting to talk to Joshua before the battle of Jericho that would rescue Rahab.

Joshua 5:13-15

Now when Joshua was near Jericho, he looked up and saw a man standing in front of him with a drawn sword in his hand. Joshua went up to him and asked, "Are you for us or for our enemies?"

"Neither," he replied, "but as commander of the army of the LORD I have now come." Then Joshua fell facedown to the ground in reverence, and asked him, "What message does my LORD have for his servant?"

The commander of the LORD's army replied, "Take off your sandals, for the place where you are standing is holy." And Joshua did so.

Joshua is understandably concerned when he sees an armed man in a threatening posture standing between him and the city he is commanded to besiege. After all, the city of Jericho is barricaded with no one coming in or out, so who could this lone man be? Joshua's question is one of alle- giances—will he have to kill this man to get to Jericho?

The being identifies Himself as the "commander of the LORD's army," a term that is very similar to a term the Old Testament prophets used to describe God—"LORD of Hosts." The term hosts is a military term that literally means "army" and refers to the heavenly and angelic powers that God alone commands.

It is no wonder that Joshua falls flat on his face in fear and reverence. The Being accepts his worship, and echoes what

God said to Moses who likewise was commanded to take off his sandals in a place made holy by the presence of the Almighty. Though He is not called the *Angel of the Lord* in this theophany to Joshua, obviously Deity is present.

The children of the people storming the city would fall into apostasy, but all God ever said about Rahab commended her exemplary faith.

I have heard people express dismay at the fact that the Lord didn't convey any "information" to Joshua. No preview of the battle, no inside information about the enemy, not even anything that was, on the surface at least, warm and encouraging. But apparently, what He said was enough to satisfy Joshua and make him certain of the holiness of the place and the gravity of the task ahead of him.

My husband Dan supplied an insight that has made this enigmatic incident make sense.

"If that is Jesus standing outside the walls of Jericho, He of course had a vested interest in the Israelites who would storm the city," Dan explained. "Those were His covenant people. But He also would have been quite concerned about the city of Jericho because of Rahab. After all, His great-grandmother many times removed was in that city. He certainly would have wanted to protect His own ancestor!"

The children of the people storming the city would fall into apostasy, but all God ever said about Rahab commended her exemplary faith.

Perhaps the incident with the *Angel of the Lord* outside the walls of Jericho was all about Rahab. Again we see the status of a faithful woman in the eyes of a God who would personally oversee a battle whose outcome would save her life. With limitless supernatural power (and surely it was the army of the Lord, not the shouting of puny men that would bring down the mighty walls) He stood guard to make sure her rescue would be secured.

Chapter 10

How Did She Do It?

 Though we don't know a single detail of how it was that Rahab kept her extended family inside her home for several weeks, we do know that she somehow managed to accomplish this. If you've ever had a big family reunion, imagine the tensions of one held in cramped quarters, with no deadline for finishing it, with the threat of a violent death hanging over you, and you'll have some idea of the physical and emotional dynamics with which Rahab had to deal.

After all, her story is not just about the rescue of one woman from a city under attack—it's about a family. When she bartered with the two spies, she'd done so not just for herself, but for all her loved ones. Surely the essence of Malachi's message in chapter 4 verse 6—the last verse in the Old Testament—was in Rahab, for through her, God had turned the hearts of the fathers to their children and the hearts of the children to their fathers. From the beginning, Rahab refused to be saved alone.

We learn in the Bible that her faith was honored when an Israelite man named Salmon married her after the fall of Jericho, and from that marriage came Boaz, the chivalrous man who married Ruth, who like Rahab had been born outside the covenant people. The son of Ruth and Boaz was Obed, who was the father of Jesse, who was the father of the famous King David. So not only was Rahab's immediate family saved from destruction, she may have even lived to see one of her descendants on the throne of Israel.

After all, her story is not just about the rescue of one woman from a city under attack—it's about a family.

For generations, her family would have treasured the story of her faith. But how in the world did she manage to keep her father, her mother, her brothers and sisters, and all their families inside her house?

We don't know her words, but we know she must have somehow persuaded them to stay. We don't know the words, but we see the results. What, without her faith and her powers of persuasion, would have meant utter loss, instead resulted in salvation and redemption.

How powerful words are! More powerful than the walls of Jericho, they protected her and her family when physical fortifications couldn't. More lasting than cities or kingdoms, they endure across centuries and cultures.

God acknowledged the power of words—just words in conversations between believers—in an astounding passage in Malachi chapter three.

"Then those who feared the LORD talked with one another, and the LORD listened and heard. A scroll of remembrance was written in his presence concerning those who feared the LORD and honored his name.

"They will be mine," says the LORD Almighty, "in the day when I make up my treasured possession. I will spare them, just as in compassion a man spares his son who serves him. And you will again see the distinction between the righteous and the wicked, between those who serve God and those who do not" (3:16-18).

The context of the passage is that some people had been saying that serving God seemed useless when all around them His opponents were prospering. And anyone in the city of Jericho could have made a strong case like this—after all, the Israelites were an exiled nomadic group with a couple of military victories that could be seen as beginners' luck. The people of Jericho, on the other hand, were the ones with the high walls and the wealth and weapons.

But to keep her family inside, Rahab must have reasoned with them about why they should stay. Like the believers in Malachi's day, she talked, and her family wasn't the only one listening. The Lord listened and heard, too. The earthly result was Rahab's family didn't panic and run, they stayed put.

But the passage in Malachi tells us that when believers talk to one another, there's a heavenly result as well. In the presence of Almighty God, a scroll was prepared with the record of those conversations that honored God, and He pronounced them, "Mine."

We're not talking about the "Book of Life" here, but a separate scroll that He keeps—sort of a coffee table book of those He's proud of, His scrapbook of those who use their tongues to honor Him, who verbally represent the facts of their lives in accordance with what He says, not what they think or even fear.

God also promised a secondary earthly result. God said that there was a coming day in which He said He would make up His "treasured possession." He would do two things for the faithful: He would spare them and He would use them as an example to others of how He makes a distinction between the righteous and the wicked.

In the world around them, where the faithless had said that serving God didn't make any difference, in that same world God would draw a line, so to speak, and show which were His and which were not. And that is exactly what happened when the walls of Jericho fell: the only ones who survived from inside those walls were those who were His.

Characteristics of Rahabic Faith

Thus we could generalize from this Malachi passage something like this: "Talking about God between believers brings about results both in heaven and on earth." Rahabic faith is inherently persuasive faith: not isolated but shared, not private but impelling and compelling to others. Though we don't know exactly how she exercised that faith in talking to her family, we know that it worked. But we also can see what that kind of persuasive faith looked like when practiced by other believers.

Persuasive faith knows facts about God's power and uses them to build faith in others. No one can build a personal, lasting faith on the emotions of others. That's why you can't get someone else to be willing to carry the cross of Christ just based on your enthusiasm. The early apostles knew this, and didn't appeal just to people's feelings or ask them to believe just to get the same kind of fervent emotional high. In fact, if you read carefully all the sermons in the book of Acts, you will find that each lesson had only one point: to convince people that Jesus was not only the long-awaited anointed Christ of God, but that He had died and been resurrected. This pivotal event in history—that a man was raised from the dead by God Himself—was attested to not only by all the apostles, but by 500 other people as well who saw the risen Christ. That event put the stamp of indisputable proof on all Jesus' teachings.

Persuasive faith doesn't try to imagine and deal with all possible unpleasant consequences.

Rahab's impassioned speech to the two spies about her utter acquiescence to God shows that she knew facts about His power in history and she would represent them as fonts of hope to her and to anyone who yielded to Him.

Persuasive faith is vulnerable to miracles and speaks of them. Rahab wasn't afraid to see the supernatural in the events of the Red Sea and in the defeat of Sihon and Og, the two kings the Israelites had defeated. She didn't believe (as do many modern theologians) that those events could be explained pragmatically as the result of a random wind drying up a swamp, or a lucky ambush against two unsuspecting enemies.

Jesus, in one of His last conversations with the disciples, tried to deal with their fears of an uncertain future. "Don't let your hearts be troubled," He advised them. If they trusted in God and in Him, they'd be protected from fear. He urged them to trust in His relationship with God. "Believe me when I say that I am in the Father and the Father is in me," He said, "or at least believe on the evidence of the miracles themselves."[80]

There's no reason for a believer to soft-pedal the mighty

miracles God has done. As Jesus pointed out, if you can't believe the words of God, then the miracles and mighty deeds He's done throughout history are powerful witnesses that can lead to faith in His words.

Persuasive faith believes God has a specific will in any situation. One of the most un-Biblical teachings circulating among Christians is that God "doesn't really care" about anything other than big decisions in your life. All the small ones are up to you, this teaching says, He will bless equally any number of options you might have. But a look at Rahab's life shows this couldn't be true: A spur-of-the-moment decision to harbor two spies who showed up at her house meant the difference between life and death for her and her family.

God does indeed have specific plans for believers. But to be able to follow those plans, you must be willing to sacrifice your own interests, give up worldly thinking, and renew your mind (and isn't that what representational thinking is all about?). Romans 12:1-2 describes this process, and concludes, "Then you will be able to test and approve what God's will is—his good, pleasing and perfect will." A believer's strong conviction that God has preferences for his or her behavior and plans will give that believer an appropriate sense of urgency and desire to figure out and follow God's will.

In conjunction with that, *persuasive faith doesn't try to re-interpret God's statements.* The very first sin ever committed on this earth happened after Eve listened to the serpent who asked her, "Did God really say, 'You must not eat from any tree in the garden'?" The serpent had three steps to getting her to sin: he first questioned what God had said, then opposed it, and then urged the woman to iconically represent the fruit in question as "good for food and pleasing to the eye"[81] instead of the way God had linguistically represented it: forbidden.

Rahab would never had been rescued if she'd used her own reasoning to try to interpret what the spies had told her about her and her family staying in the house. What would have happened if she'd thought that meant only at night? What if she'd decided that just a representative of each family had seemed appropriate, thinking that there would be plenty of time to gather everybody up while holes were being breached in the walls? What if she'd waited until she saw the Israelites drawing their weapons? All would have been lost!

Persuasive faith makes a conscious decision of risk and self-sacrifice to accept God's representations of providence over fears of loss. Trying to save your own life will lose it, Jesus said. The only way to follow Him is to deny yourself and take up a cross—a symbol of your own death—and go where He has gone.

"If anyone would come after me, he must deny himself and take up his cross and follow me. For whoever wants to save his life will lose it, but whoever loses his life for me and for the gospel will save it. What good is it for a man to gain the whole world yet forfeit his soul? Or what can a man give in exchange for his soul?"[82]

And even this process is all about words: "If anyone is ashamed of me and my words," Jesus continued, "the Son of Man will be ashamed of him when he comes in his Father's glory with the holy angels."[83]

Rahab had to make a conscious decision of risk and self-sacrifice to gather all her loved ones together. Surely whole families would have been missed at work and in social situations. Rahab was willing to face criticism and perhaps even threats, and to persuade her family to be impervious to these factors as well.

Persuasive faith doesn't try to imagine and deal with all possible unpleasant consequences. We unfortunately think it is mature and responsible to think ahead to all the unpleasant outcomes that could possibly result from our actions. Sometimes we even talk about such things in an attempt to show others we're not heedless of the dangers we might face.

However, even God limits His own thinking about certain things. In Jeremiah 19, God recounts the many kinds of sick sins that His people were involved in, including the reprehensible sin of child sacrifice, "something I did not command or mention," says God, "nor did it enter my mind" (verse 5).

Talking about how God might let us "fall through the cracks" in a bad situation is not mature—it's faithless. It's unimaginable that Rahab could have kept order and peace in her home if she'd allowed herself to speculate on failure, or if she'd allowed others to do so. If God—who has limitless power and intelligence—deliberately limits things that He thinks about, why shouldn't we?

Persuasive faith regards the passage of time as no factor in computing the fulfillment of God's promises. Abraham's example of what Romans 4:20 calls faith without "wavering" is a benchmark. Even though decades had passed since the original promise of a son, in spite of physical factors that any doctor would say prevents a pregnancy, Abraham in hope believed. In other words, for Abraham the passage of time was a fact, but its proper representation was that of an opportunity to express continued hope and belief in the promise.

> **Persuasive faith regards the passage of time as no factor in computing the fulfillment of God's promises.**

Sometimes when an "unreasonable" period of time passes between a promise of God and its fulfillment, people of weak faith waver while people of strong faith surge forward. The passage of time, I am convinced, is one of those factors that Jesus called "life's worries"[84] that keep the Word of God from maturing in the heart. But longevity of faith and unwavering hope in difficult or extended periods of time are themselves powerful witnesses that will convince others when nothing else will.

Persuasive faith doesn't need a timeline, just assurance of eventual relief. Rahab had no idea of when the spies were coming back, and couldn't reassure her family with any kind of deadline. (No advent calendar of marking of so many days till rescue, for instance, hung on her wall.) Her faith is all the more extraordinary because it was open-ended and was truly able to endure to the end without knowing *when* that would be.

How much in contrast this was to some of the Israelites, who'd had a 40-year calendar ticking away in the desert and still, with just months left on their sentence, wiped the crumbs of the miraculous bread of manna from their lips and went to eat with the Moabites and worship their god, the Baal of Peor.[85]

In the response section corresponding to this chapter, there are additional characteristics of persuasive faith, and I hope you'll take the time to explore them.

Persuasive Faith in Waiting

We are amazed at, and honor, the faith of Rahab in the way that she waited and persuaded others to do so, too. She realized the essential truth in the fact that she could not control anything that went on outside the walls of Jericho, just what went on within them and specifically within her own home. We can identify with this—how can we develop the persuasive language to convince our loved ones to stay inside the house of faith with us?

Persuasive faith doesn't need a timeline, just assurance of eventual relief.

Knowing how to wait, and how to persuade others to wait, is a precious and rare skill. The Old Testament recounts, over and over, how people refused to wait on God and chose to act, lapsing eventually into further sin and unbelief. And no one can read the New Testament—especially the epistles and the Revelation—without tasting the earnest yearning of God's people as they anxiously await the return of Jesus.

Rahab waited, and persuaded others to wait, too. You're in good company, oh patient waiter upon God. Use all your persuasive powers to convince all those you love to stay in the place of safety He has set for you, in His church. He will surely come for you.

Chapter 11

A God Who Goes in Circles

Imagine, if you will, that Rahab's window opened toward the Israelite camp, and that she could see them in the distance. There's no doubt she believed the promises of the spies, and through the hours, days, and weeks she stayed incommunicado in her house in Jericho with her relatives, perhaps she speculated on how her rescue would be played out.

Imagine her excitement when the waters of the mighty Jordan River piled up miles upstream, and she could see the pageantry and spectacle of the priests stepping into the river, bearing the ark of the covenant. Then, the image of hundreds of thousands of people that crossed that river, some cavorting and skipping like children at the prospect of walking in the raging river's dry bed, some glancing fearfully upstream and hurrying across before God changed His mind, some marching resolutely forward, eyes fixed on the land of promise before them.

"Yes, that's right," Rahab must have thought, "God is doing just exactly what He did forty years ago. He is God of heaven and everything on earth. I was right about that—He is with this people. I did the right thing risking everything to be part of them."

How Rahab must have wondered why twelve men took those large stones from the river bed and piled them up at the shore, and why people filed silently past them, fathers holding their children and pointing to the mound of rocks as if they meant something more than just their river-worn smoothness. She couldn't know the meaning of these facts, these visual icons, without a verbal representation.[86] Perhaps—she might have thought—they were for catapults to launch against the impenetrable walls of the city, or another, unknown weaponry.

Perhaps Rahab would have been the only person in that fear-wrenched city who had a window on the wall and had the courage to put her head and neck out the window, waving the red cord.

"Time must be close," she would have wanted to tell her mom and dad. "Nobody go outside. See, the army is on the move." And indeed, anyone who saw the events of that day would have been frantic with excitement and anticipation, and Joshua 5:1 tells us that this single event made every king up and down the entire coast of the land sick with fear: "their hearts melted and they no longer had the courage to face the Israelites."

With such a psychological advantage, surely the Israelites would move forward.

Imagine what would have been in Rahab's mind when the production of flint knives began. "Good, more weapons, good thinking," she may have mused. But imagine her confusion when Joshua, the mighty leader of the Israelites, lined up every last adult male—the whole fighting force of the army—and used those razor-sharp implements to cut a little piece of flesh off the most sensitive part of their bodies. It took days for the men, walking spraddle-legged, to heal.

"Yeah, that's real war-like," some of her brothers may have said. "That's going to make them better fighters?"

How did Rahab convince them to stay inside when, four days later, they celebrated the Passover? She couldn't have known about the significance of the lamb, the blood over the lintels, the unleavened bread of haste.

With all the gathering of herbs and vegetables, the making of bread and the roasting of sheep on spits over thousands of firepits, it must have looked for all the world like a barbecue there on the banks of the Jordan.

And then Joshua's mysterious encounter with the Stranger near Jericho, where the leader of this vast army bowed before

102

Someone (and she couldn't have known this) with an even greater, invisible army. Who were these men, she may have wondered, and why was one worshiping the other?

But the next morning dawned, and Joshua had an announcement. At his command, all the armed men lined up in ranks. Behind them, seven white-clad priests hefted hollowed-out rams horns onto their shoulders, and behind them other priests gingerly lifted the poles carrying a mysterious, draped box. Another armed guard filed in behind the ark of the covenant. All in all, over 600,000 men assembled.

Joshua 6:1-13

Now Jericho was tightly shut up because of the Israelites. No one went out and no one came in.

Then the LORD said to Joshua, "See, I have delivered Jericho into your hands, along with its king and its fighting men. March around the city once with all the armed men. Do this for six days. Have seven priests carry trumpets of rams' horns in front of the ark. On the seventh day, march around the city seven times, with the priests blowing the trumpets. When you hear them sound a long blast on the trumpets, have all the people give a loud shout; then the wall of the city will collapse and the people will go up, every man straight in."

So Joshua son of Nun called the priests and said to them, "Take up the ark of the covenant of the LORD and have seven priests carry trumpets in front of it." And he ordered the people, "Advance! March around the city, with the armed guard going ahead of the ark of the LORD."

When Joshua had spoken to the people, the seven priests carrying the seven trumpets before the LORD went forward, blowing their trumpets, and the ark of the LORD's covenant followed them. The armed guard marched ahead of the priests who blew the trumpets, and the rear guard followed the ark. All this time the trumpets were sounding. But Joshua had commanded the people, "Do not give a war cry, do not raise your voices, do not say a word until the day I tell you to shout. Then shout!" So he had the ark of the LORD carried around the city, circling it once. Then the people returned to camp and spent the night there.

Joshua got up early the next morning and the priests took up the ark of the LORD. The seven priests carrying the seven trumpets went forward, marching before the ark of the LORD and blowing the trumpets. The armed men went ahead of them and the rear guard followed the ark of the LORD, while the trumpets kept sounding.

Imagine Rahab's excitement! They were here! They'd come to rescue her, just as they promised! How she must have strained her eyes to see if any of those armed men were the young spies she had harbored. Would they remember their promises?

Perhaps Rahab would have been the only person in that fear-wrenched city who had a window on the wall and had the courage to put her head and neck out the window, waving the red cord. Surely the armies saw the cord.

With over 600,000 men marching, just the sound of trudging feet in the dirt must have been thunderous. And then there was the plaintive, unearthly sound of the ram's horns that hung in the air, ominous and chilling. But no words, no battle cries, no other sounds.

Depending on the width of the ranks of men, they may have completely circled the city. The tension among the people inside must have been unbearable. Something was about to happen.

Something did. Its circuit completed, the front line of the forward guard wheeled away from the city wall, and without a single word, the entire army marched back to their camp and went to bed for the night.

Rahab must have been devastated. "What was that all about?"

"Maybe it was just a reconnaissance trip, checking out the terrain, a dry run."

So on the second day they marched around the city once and returned to the camp.

6:14a

104

Inside Rahab's house, the questions must have flown like arrows. "Why did the armies march around again?" "Did they just need a second look?" "And why did they not carry any of the necessary implements to take a city with such high thick walls?" "Why no battering rams?" "Why no ladders to scale the walls?" "And no digging implements or bricks to build siege ramps?"

They did this for six days.
6:14b

The third day, they marched around mute, and then went home.

The fourth day, they marched around the city and then went home.

The fifth day, they marched around the city and then went home.

The sixth day, they marched around the city and then went home.

The scoffing must have begun, first as whispers, then as accusations. Mother and Dad must have tried to reason with Rahab.

"Look, dear, you're a whore. And men always tell whores, 'You don't belong in this place. I have to leave, but don't worry, honey, I'll come back for you.' And then they never do. Men have been breaking those kinds of promises to women like you since time began. So don't take it personally."

But Rahab *had* taken it personally—life or death personally.

Somehow she managed to quell the fears, handle the questions, convince them all. And good thing she did convince them to stay put, for the next day was going to be the most nerve-wracking of all.

On the seventh day, they got up at daybreak and marched around the city seven times in the same manner, except that on that day they circled the city seven times.
6:15

If there is one mental image I have of Rahab that exactly personifies her to me, it would be of her face, framed by the window of her hope, as she watched the scenes of armed men circling her city, a face resolute in faith.

If there's one thing she could have known about the God of the Israelites other than His enormous power, it would have been that He did things His way. He had made His own people wander 40 years on what should have been a 40-day journey. What she probably didn't know were other similar instances in their history—such as the time that God had His people circle around the hill country of Seir until He said, "Enough" and sent them to the north.[87] The issue, for the Israelites, was whether they would be led step by step by God, and they repeatedly showed that in spite of overt guidance, they still mistrusted God.[88] (Rahab didn't have a cloud or pillar of fire nor any periodic personal assurances from a representative of God, yet she managed to trust Him—another reason God valued her so highly.)

The army that marched before her had learned the hard lessons of the desert. Why were 600,000 men able to march in absolute silence for seven days, without arguing, without questions? They'd learned that God can silence rebellion, for every soldier there was an orphan of disobedient parents. And they'd learned another hard lesson: there are no "pre-conditions" that must be in place for God to accomplish His purposes. He didn't need the Israelites' physical strength to oppose the Red Sea or the Jordan or the walls of Jericho. He didn't need their wealth or their intelligence or their opinions. All He needed was for them to cooperate long enough that He could show the world what He would do for a group of people that would obey Him.

And if it took seven days of walking in circles for them to prove to themselves that they could, just for a while, for once in their history, keep their mouths shut before Him, then He graciously gave them that.

The Ministry of Waiting

We often think of a ministry as an activity. Witnessing, serving, teaching, leading: these are ministries that can be activities, but in waiting all are exemplified and perfected. Most of our lives, percentage-wise, are not spent in doing, but in waiting; not in proving but in the pre-proof stage of testing.

We're called on to do more waiting than anything else. I've heard it said, and I think it must be true, that the most oft-repeated commandment in the Bible is, "Wait on the Lord." But lest we think that this is an onerous task laid on our shoulders alone, look at the way God waits for us.

Most of our lives, percentage-wise, are not spent in doing, but in waiting; not in proving but in the pre-proof stage of testing.

One of the most winsome characteristics of God is seen in the way He waited on humans who wanted to do something to honor Him. We saw in the chapter, "The Ancient Voice of Jesus," for instance, how the Lord waited on people to cook Him meals[89]—He, who doesn't need food, just hung around to let them show their gratitude and affection.

We often talk of waiting on the Lord and even whine about the fact that we don't know when God is going to act on our behalf, to give us justice against our adversaries and reward us by what we ask for. But consider Jesus, the Author and Perfecter of our faith. For two thousand years, He's been waiting for *His* enemies to be made His footstool.[90] And talk about being left out of the loop on deadlines—He understands what it's like not to have a date and time. He doesn't know when He's coming back to earth.[91]

We follow in the shadow of a waiting Jesus when we wait. Like Rahab, we can trust Him, not only with what we can see and understand, but also with what we can't see and don't understand.

And also like Rahab, we have to operate on an underlying assumption that is the basis for all our thinking: the assumption that no matter how it may look, God is not going around in meaningless circles in our lives, He's doing something for faithful people.

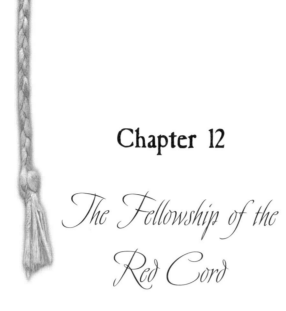

Chapter 12

The Fellowship of the Red Cord

Joshua 6:15-25

On the seventh day, they got up at daybreak and marched around the city seven times in the same manner, except that on that day they circled the city seven times. The seventh time around, when the priests sounded the trumpet blast, Joshua commanded the people, "Shout! For the LORD has given you the city! The city and all that is in it are to be devoted to the LORD. Only Rahab the prostitute and all who are with her in her house shall be spared, because she hid the spies we sent.

"But keep away from the devoted things, so that you will not bring about your own destruction by taking any of them. Otherwise you will make the camp of Israel liable to destruction and bring trouble on it. All the silver and gold and the articles of bronze and iron are sacred to the LORD and must go into his treasury."

When the trumpets sounded, the people shouted, and at the sound of the trumpet, when the people gave a loud shout, the wall collapsed; so every man charged straight in, and they took the city. They devoted the city to the LORD and destroyed with the sword every living thing in it—men and women, young and old, cattle, sheep and donkeys.

Joshua said to the two men who had spied out the land, "Go into the prostitute's house and bring her out and all who belong to her, in accordance with your oath to her." So the young men who had done the spying went in and brought out Rahab, her father and mother and brothers and all who belonged to her. They brought out her entire family and put them in a place outside the camp of Israel. Then they burned the whole city and everything in it, but they put the silver and gold and the articles of bronze and iron into the treasury of the LORD's house. But Joshua spared Rahab the prostitute, with her family and all who belonged to her, because she hid the men Joshua had sent as spies to Jericho—and she lives among the Israelites to this day.

Ah, we love happy endings and dilemmas that have solutions. That's why mystery stories sell so well, why puzzles have to be solve-able to satisfy. The Bible is a book of solved problems and satisfactory endings to stories, where people get their just deserts: if not here on earth, at least in heaven justice is satisfied.

What is the story of Rahab about? It's about whether or not people will accept words from God instead of their own experiences.

But we don't live lives of solved problems. And even the predicaments we get ourselves into that God solves for us aren't the issues that our minds dwell on—it's the present quandries that keep us up at night, not the resolved situations of the past. We live right in the middle of the story of Rahab, in seemingly open-ended situations with no deadline for relief.

We love the story of Rahab because she's rescued by the two white knights who carry her away to a land of milk and honey. We love the story of Joseph in the book of Genesis because he saves his family and gets a little sweet revenge to boot. We love the book of Job because he gets back double of all he lost. And don't forget the resurrected Jesus—sitting at the right hand of the Father, able to set everything right.

But look more carefully at the number of words used to describe these people's situations in Scripture. In general, we see more of their trials than we do their triumphs. Looking at frustration is frustrating, so we skip over it. We don't want to enter into the thought world of Joseph as he sits overnight in a pit as his brothers plot to kill him and then decide just to sell him away as a slave; or the 750 days he spent in a stifling Egyptian prison. Most of what we know of Job is his bewilderment at why one day he's rich and the next he's sitting on an ash heap scraping open sores with a piece of pottery. And Jesus put up with ignorance, jealousy, greed, and misunderstanding for 33 years and then dies naked and disgraced, forsaken even by God.

And Rahab—for most of the time we know her, she's either risking her neck or wracking her nerves waiting to be rescued.

Most of us know less about the risk part, but we can surely identify with the waiting. And how our hearts crave the kind of resolution she received. That's why her story satisfies us at such a deep level. In reading Scripture, we have in her story and so many others the luxury of God's vantage point, knowing that it turns out okay.

What is the story of Rahab about? It's about the deliberate decision to put physical factors of life—things like high walls and military might and political strength—in perspective.

Rahab is one of that "cloud of witnesses" of Hebrews 12:1 who enable us today to throw off entanglements and sin and to be able to run the race of faith, right to the finish line. Her story is like Jonah in the great fish, redemption even when swallowed up by the consequences of our sins. It is like the resurrection of Jesus, life out of hopeless death. It is like our own coming resurrection, when somebody will come and take us away from the Jerichos of our own deaths.

What is the story of Rahab about? Well, as much as it is about the story of a woman of faith, it is as much about the faithlessness of the Israelites against whose blackness of rebellion she shines like a diamond in sunlight. The Israelites were the ones with all the miracles, all the provision, all the words from God Himself. She knew nothing but His awesome power, and that was enough for her.

And lest we rush to judgment of the Israelites of her day— how many more promises, laws, provisions, and prophesies do we have in a complete book of His mighty deeds? And a personal Savior who died to rescue us!

What is the story of Rahab about? It's about whether or not people will accept words from God instead of their own experiences. Really, we can identify more exactly with the family of Rahab than we can the woman herself: she actually talked to the spies, got the promises firsthand. We, like her brothers, sisters, parents, and other kin, have to take someone's word for what the promises are.

Jesus addressed very issue when He told Thomas (the one who wouldn't believe unless he could put his fingers in the resurrected Lord's wounds) that first-hand belief is commendable, but second-hand belief—that which must rely on the words of the witnesses—is *blessed.*[92]

What is the story of Rahab about? It's about the deliberate decision to put physical factors of life—things like high walls and military might and political strength—in perspective. It means that any believer must make *all* physical factors relative to the expressed will of God. The deciding factor in any battle a Christian faces is not his or her personal strength and competence to fight the battle, but the will of God in the matter.

It wasn't psychological warfare or sound waves from ram's horns that brought down those massive walls. It was the decision of God, and nothing opposes that. His will is the invisible power that sustains everything from the inside out and keeps all creation from collapse.[93] It wasn't just that the walls were struck by anything, it was as much that God removed their ability to stand: they "collapsed."

There was a treasure inside those walls, walls that fell outward instead of inward so as to protect that priceless gem. Paul speaks of a similar treasure in earthen vessels in 2 Corinthians chapter 4. Our faith resides in the fragile pottery of our bodies, only kept from collapse by the equalizing pressure of Christ in us. We are maintained and sustained by that, and that alone.

All physical obstacles are canceled out by the promises of God and His ability and willingness to keep those promises. All our eggs are put in the one basket of trust in Him and a willingness to be part of a continuum of faith. We appropriate as if our very own the experiences of people in Scripture. We say with the Israelites that God led us through the Red Sea, with David that we've been saved from bears and lions and Philistines, with Paul that we have been crucified with Christ and no longer live, but He lives in us.

What is the story of Rahab about? It portrays a no-nonsense God who won't take sides except against the faithless, and who levels the ground of His favor based on active trust in Himself alone. By active trust I mean not only faith in Him that doesn't question His character, motives or actions; but also faith that either acts or waits according to instructions. That level ground means that all outsiders could join up with the Israelites and be rewarded along with them as long as they entered into covenant with God too.[94] It means that when any of them sinned, if they would seek God with all their hearts, He would be found by them,[95] for He would not withhold Himself from a repentant, searching heart. And that level ground meant that any alien among them should be treated with grace and compassion, because this God of love reminded them, "you are to love those who are aliens, for you yourselves were aliens in Egypt."[96]

> **What is the story of Rahab about? It is about how God views, and uses, the leftovers of society.**

What is the story of Rahab about? It is about how God views, and uses, the leftovers of society. The Canaanite woman we've referred to so often from Matthew 15:21-28 didn't care that the healing of her child would be compared to crumbs that fall from a table instead of the whole meal. All she needed was a healing, and she didn't mind bantering, cajoling, retorting—anything to persuade. Jesus called this kind of faith "great."

Perhaps she had seen five thousand people fed and counted the twelve basketfuls of leftovers and had concluded that it didn't matter if you got fed the first time around or with what was left—you wouldn't starve that way. Rahab reasoned the same way. It didn't matter if she saved her family from within a pagan city or marching outside it. The end result was they'd all be saved.

One of the most significant generalizations from the life of Rahab the prostitute is that God wants unflinching faith, and He'll take it wherever He can get it. In her, He canonized one of the greatest truths of all time: No matter who you are, no matter what you've done, your present faith carries more weight with Him than all your past sins.

What is the story of Rahab about? At the most fundamental level, it addresses an issue of supreme importance: that of security. On that date in ancient history, the most dangerous place in the whole world was on the wall of Jericho—unless you were a woman with a promise of divine protection. The only part of that wall that remained standing was what was necessary to keep Rahab's house upright.

What was disaster for everyone else inside that city, was salvation for her and her family. What was utter loss for those who only feared and did not believe, was reward and honor for a hardscrabble woman and her loved ones she wrangled into quiescence.

Another generalization is clear: The place that might seem most dangerous is the safest if God has put you there.

The story is told by Tony Evans in the book *No More Excuses* of the runaway slave Frederick Nolen who had run all day from the men pursing him. Out of exhaustion he hid overnight in a cave. The next morning, when the men who were chasing him came to the cave, they reasoned that no one could possibly be in there because of the great spider web that covered the mouth of the cave, spun there overnight by an industrious spider. They continued looking for Nolen elsewhere, but they never caught him.

Nolen concluded, "Where God is, a spider's web is like a wall. Where God is not, a wall is like a spider's web."

In the same way, the wall that surrounded Jericho, on which its inhabitants had depended to protect them, was no obstacle to God. Similarly, the wall attached to the window where there was a red cord was protected by that flimsy symbol. The red cord of her hope was the strongest, most indestructible substance in the world.

We shouldn't be surprised that something that was far more

significant than a mere military campaign—the gifting according to ancient promise of a land of inheritance to Abraham's descendants—was held up just for one woman of faith. I once heard someone speculate, "Who knows if the world is being kept from nuclear war because of the prayers of one paralytic in a nursing home, in constant prayer?" God has promised that coming days of great worldwide anguish will actually be shortened, for the sake of chosen believers.[97] It seems that there's no perceptible limit to what God can do if people just ask and believe.

It's through Rahabic faith that people—men and women alike—have conquered kingdoms, administered justice, shut the mouths of lions, quenched the fury of flames, and escaped the edge of the sword; for in faith weakness is turned to strength.[98] All that made Rahab sinful—her accessibility to men who were strangers, her come-and-go house, her conniving mind—all these weaknesses were her strengths because of her faith in a God who could change her life.

The story of Rahab is about a God who just keeps trying, over and over, generation after generation, to get His people to agree to a covenant of love where He does all the work and we just love Him and those around us.[99] We know that the generation that left Egypt had been unfaithful, and with sorrow we read that the generation that *followed* the conquerors of Jericho—the children of those who marched around the city— abandoned their fathers' faith and ignored all God had done for them.[100] They chose the facts of their rich surroundings over the representations of God's past mighty deeds and His requirements for their well-being.

It's a see-saw all the way through the Old Testament: Adam is faithful, then he sins. A world full of wickedness is swept away by a flood, and Noah's children blow it. Abraham receives promises, and his children begin wars that are still bursting out in flames in the Near East today. Moses rescues the people, and they rebel in the desert. Jericho falls, and a generation later so do the Israelite children. Judges come and go, kings reign and despoil, the nation is carried into captivity where they repent and 70 years later they return. They give up idols, bemoan His silence for 400 years; and then sell out their Messiah as fast as they can. It becomes an almost-laughable axiom: the nicer God treats people, the faster they run away from Him.

Why does He keep trying? Why does He do it again in the twenty-first century?

The real scarlet cord of our lives must be the reality of the blood of Jesus that streamed down the cross—our only hope for salvation.

He does it because He just can't help Himself. He's a God of mercy and forgiveness. He keeps loving the *idea of people* even when individuals treat Him like dirt. Every morning, He looks with fresh new eyes on the earth, searching out anybody who'll listen to Him and love Him.[101]

One day thousands of years ago, He found such a person. Her name was Rahab.

This book, her story, came with a red cord. It is a representation of some truths that have endured for these thousands of years.

It means, "I'll hold on to the promises of God, no matter what."

"If I lose this cord, it doesn't matter—I'll get another cord, but the promises stand."

"I'll trust Him no matter how things look around me: I'll take His representations over my own every day of my life."

Rahab really lived. The book of Joshua says that "she lives among the Israelites to this day," and even in the twenty-first century she still lives through the words of God that have outlasted her weary bones. We have a connection with her, a kind of fellowship of the red cord that spans all those years.

She sat inside a window of desperation, where men came to pay for the words and actions of love. She risked everything for another set of words, the promises the men made her, the "don't worry, honey, we're coming back for you" banter of departing backs, the big kiss-off. She *knew* that men play mind games with prostitutes. She *knew* people make promises to get what they want, and then they leave. But she believed in their God.

We sit inside our own windows of emotions that range from

uneasiness to sheer panic, and we throw a cord outside our windows. We, too, live on the basis of promises by a Man who came to our sinful world and then left, assuring us that He'd be back. But He gave us no timetable either. He knows we're as sinful as any prostitute—after all, all sin is equal to Him, all separates us from the Father.

Many times it must look to us like His actions aren't very productive. Why does He do things like pile up rocks in our lives? Why the flint knives and barbecues? And what about the fact that so many times God seems just to be moving in circles in our lives, not going anywhere, not noticing us?

We too, have been given the responsibility to try with all our powers to persuade our families to stay in the only truly safe place—within His kingdom that is constantly under siege. Somehow we must convince our loved ones that His promise is worth risking everything for.

Jesus left us with the Holy Spirit—a "down payment" on those promises. *The real scarlet cord of our lives must be the reality of the blood of Jesus that streamed down the cross—our only hope for salvation.*

But we must be brave enough to display it, talk about it, live on its reality.

Because honey, He's coming back, for you!

Part Two:

The View out Your Window

Chapter Response Section

Introduction

 As you will see, Rahab sat for what must have seemed like an eternity waiting for God to fulfill His promises. Each of us sits by a figurative window of our lives as well; waiting for that unanswered prayer, that as-yet-unfulfilled promise, that supreme test of our faith and ability to wait.

What is the view from your window? How are you representing the promises of God and the events that surround you?

Studying the story of Rahab is stimulating and helpful, but don't let it become a mirror into which you look and then walk away, forgetting what you look like.[102] The Bible promises great blessings to those who learn from the examples of people like Rahab.

In this response section, there is a chapter corresponding to each chapter of the first section of the book. After you read the Rahab section, you can come here and reflect on and put into action what you've learned from her example.

You may learn new terms, stretch your mind, see things as you've never seen them before. The benefit you derive will be exactly proportional to the amount of thought, effort, and prayer that you put into these responses.

Chapter One Response

Most often the story of the conquest of Jericho is told from the point of view of the Israelites. Fill out the following chart to ascertain what Rahab was doing during the events of Joshua chapters 2 through 6.

If there is not an answer in Scripture for a part of the chart, leave it blank or put in question marks.

What Israelites Were Doing	Amount of Time that Transpired	What Rahab Was Doing/How She Responded
Spies come to Rahab's house		
Spies are sought by king		
Spies talk to Rahab		
Spies escape out wall		
Spies hide in hills		
Spies report to Joshua		
Spies spend time in camp		
Crossing of the Jordan		
Rocks put on the shore		
Circumcision reinstituted		
Healing from circumcision		
Passover preparations		
Passover celebrated		
"Man" with drawn sword talks to Joshua		
First march around city		
Second march around city		

What Israelites Were Doing	Amount of Time that Transpired	What Rahab Was Doing/How She Responded
Third march around city		
Fourth march around city		
Fifth march around city		
Sixth march around city		
Seventh march around city		

Focus Summary

If you're familiar with the story of the crossing of the Jordan and the falling of Jericho, you may not have considered how all the events of that episode affected Rahab as she waited inside Jericho. Her only option was to stay put and wait on the Lord—a seemingly passive posture that turned out to be an act of great faith.

Chapter Two Response

One of the skills that you will learn as you proceed with the story of Rahab is a skill we call *generalizing*. A generalization is a principle obtained from reading a Scriptural passage. In *one* sense it is *a conclusion that you would reach about the way God works with people*, a conclusion drawn from the passage you are reading. Of course any generalization must be true to all of Scripture. You wouldn't legitimately be able to generalize that God always saves inexperienced soldiers by reading the story of David and Goliath, for instance. But you could legitimately say that when God has announced a purpose (like when He had Samuel anoint David king of Israel when he was just a youngster), He will protect the person who knows God's will for himself or herself.

So, in this case, a good generalization concerning the battle of David and Goliath might be: *Strength and experience can't save someone who is opposing the will of God.*

Or another might be: *No matter how formidable a believer's opponent, that opponent will ultimately be defeated by God and not by personal power.*

Another might be: *God often shows His great power by using people and instruments that the world would see as unlikely for the purpose.*

Get the idea?

So, here are some generalizations about Rahab from Chapter One.

God has great respect for a woman of faith, and will move around even political events like wars to benefit such a woman.

As the number of spies sent to Jericho shows, a few people with great faith are of more use to God and more helpful to His people than many people who are filled with fear.

Now, you formulate a generalization from the life of Rahab about how God views someone with a disreputable past that turns to Him in complete faith:

The *second* important element of a generalization is *the way it can be used in your life.* Very few of us are going to go to battle against a nine-foot giant or be called upon to wait patiently inside a walled city that will fall in battle. But we can take the generalizations and apply them to our own lives.

Write out how you might, in a situation you are currently facing, be able to apply these generalizations:

God has great respect for a woman of faith, and will move around even political events like wars to benefit such a woman.

What that means for my life is . . .

_____

_____

_____

_____

_____

As the number of spies sent to Jericho shows, a few people with great faith are of more use to God and more helpful to His people than many people who are filled with fear.

What that means for my life is . . .

_____

_____

_____

_____

_____

Now use the generalization, about how God views someone with a disreputable past, that you wrote above.

What that means for my life is . . .

_____

_____

_____

_____

Another concept introduced in Chapter Two is the idea of facts and representations.

A fact is any element that surrounds us in our lives on this earth. A person is a fact, an event is a fact, an object like a table is a fact, and a condition like an illness is a fact.

A representation is the way that you access that fact. You don't carry other people around in your head, but you have memories of how they look and what they say. Those are representations of the people, who are facts.

You aren't able to really "relive" any events, but you access past events through your memory of them. Those memories are representations. You know about your kitchen table even when you're at the grocery store—you have a visual representation of that table in your mind. Even conditions like illness aren't just in your body, but in the way that your brain processes the information from your nerve endings.

Much of the time we access the facts of our world by representing them in words. I can say the words "George Washington" to you and you will "see" a white-haired man and think of his role in founding the United States of America. But he's been dead almost 200 years, strictly speaking as a fact. But my verbal representation of him, just words, brings him to mind for you.

Write in your own words what is the difference between a fact and a representation.

_____

_____

_____

_____

_____

Give an example of a fact and a representation of it.

_____

_____

_____

_____

Now, here's where the rubber meets the road for Christians. We all have facts that surround us, and we usually represent those facts with language. For instance, we may have undergone some trauma as a child. That event, that fact, has passed away, but we continue to represent it by talking about it.

Write down an event or condition from your childhood or past, one that you believe deeply affected you, that you often talk about.

Read Romans 8:28 and write a generalization from it.

If God were speaking about your past experience that deeply affected you, what would He say about it in light of Romans 8:28?

How do you usually talk about (represent) that past fact or event?

_____

_____

_____

_____

_____

Focus Summary

A fact (a person, place, thing, event, or circumstance) is not the same as the representations through which we access that fact. We have a choice as to how to represent the circumstances of our lives. But for Christians, we must represent them as God does, not just as our experience or feelings would dictate.

Chapter Three Response

Generalizing from Scripture about the Role of Personal Experience

When Rahab encountered the two young men who had come to her home and hid them, she met people of great faith whom she saw as God's representatives. Since these were young men (Joshua 6:23), they had not experienced the crossing of the Red Sea. Yet they are willing to take on a dangerous spy mission to expedite what they see as an inevitability: The city of Jericho will fall, and they are prepared to keep their promise to the woman who will help them escape the city to report back to Joshua.

Rahab certainly did not experience the crossing of the Red Sea, and yet she is more respectful of the God of Israel than the people who had actually experienced it, as Joshua 2:8-10 shows.

What is the first thing that Rahab tells the spies that indicates she believes her city and country will be conquered by the Israelites?

_____

_____

_____

_____

What is the emotional climate in Jericho?

_____

_____

_____

In what way are Rahab's emotions like those of her countrymen?

_____

_____

_____

129

What does Rahab say is the source of the military strength of the Israelites?

_____

_____

_____

_____

_____

What does Rahab say about God that contrasts with what the ten frightened spies had said almost 40 years before (Numbers 13:26-33)?

_____

_____

_____

_____

_____

What did she say that agreed with what Caleb said?

_____

_____

_____

_____

_____

Read Numbers 14:6-9 and write a generalization about the potential success of a project which the Lord wants to be successful.

_____

_____

_____

_____

_____

Write a generalization from that same passage about the relative strength of obstacles that might oppose projects that the Lord instigates.

_____

_____

_____

_____

_____

Looking at Personal Experience

Many people believe that they have to have personally experienced something in order to believe it's true. For instance, many people have concluded that God is uncaring because they have undergone painful circumstances.

The role of personal experience is powerful. In the New Testament, we read that one of the disciples, Thomas, did not see Jesus after He was resurrected and refused to believe the accounts of the others (John 20:31). Unless he could put his hands into Jesus' side and touch the nailprints, he said, he would not believe.

Write a generalization about the role of personal experience versus belief in what the Bible says about Jesus from John 20:29-33.

_____

_____

_____

_____

_____

How was the faith of those who crossed the Red Sea affected by that dramatic experience?

_____

_____

_____

How was Rahab's assessment of God formed by hearing about the Red Sea?

_____

_____

_____

_____

_____

Focus Summary

Each Christian must decide whether our own personal experience and how we feel about it, or the representations of God and His working of power as revealed in Scripture, will be the basis of how we assess the character of God. Faith, therefore, would be demonstrated in the wholehearted acceptance of God's representations—*especially when they conflict with our own experiences and feelings.*

Chapter Four Response

In Chapter Four, we saw how Rahab used the past actions of God as a narrative base for assessing a situation and her options in it.

1) What is the biggest challenge facing you in your life right now? (Examples: marital situation, job uncertainty, or problems with children.)

2) Think back to the last time that you discussed this challenge with someone else. What percentage of your conversation or discussion used the past actions of God (which you know about from Scripture) as a narrative base for your discourse?

3) What would you say was the biggest contributing factor to your narrative base that is revealed in the way you talk about this situation?

4) In Romans 1:20, it says, "For since the creation of the world God's invisible qualities—his eternal power and divine nature—have been clearly seen, being understood from what has been made, so that men are without excuse."

The first aspect, God's divine power, was something Rahab understood very well. However, she may not have known very much about His nature. What did the spies say to her in Joshua 2:14, as representatives of God, that would have told her something about His nature?

_____

_____

_____

_____

_____

_____

5) From the moment the spies promised Rahab that they'd come back and rescue her and her loved ones, that promise became part of her narrative base (as her subsequent actions clearly show). Because of this narrative base, what "options" might Rahab have thought to exercise, actions that were therefore precluded by the fact that she had a promise? (Here's one to get you started: she couldn't give in to the same mindless fear as the rest of the city of Jericho, because she knew she was going to be rescued.)

_____

_____

_____

_____

_____

_____

_____

6) In Genesis chapter 32, Jacob was going out to meet his brother Esau. There had been bad blood between the two since the time that Jacob had wrangled his brother out of his birthright, and then deceived their father into giving himself a great blessing and Esau a lesser one.

Jacob was right to be afraid of how his meeting with Esau would turn out. Look at Jacob's prayer in Genesis 32:9-12. How did the prior promises of God to Jacob form his narrative base that we see in this prayer?

---

7) Read Genesis 33:1-20. How did Jacob's meeting with Esau turn out?

---

8) Read carefully John chapters 15–17. Make a list of the blessings that a believer can expect from the Lord.

9) Go back and re-read John 17:20-23. How do we know that the assurances you just listed weren't just for believers of Jesus' day?

_____

_____

_____

_____

_____

10) Choose two of the promises or assurances that you listed in question number 6 and write how you can incorporate Jesus' words into your narrative base concerning the challenge that you listed in question number 1.

_____

_____

_____

_____

_____

_____

_____

11) What "options" might you otherwise have, in your difficult situation, that would be precluded by the fact that you have promises and assurances from the Lord?

_____

_____

_____

_____

_____

12) In what specific ways can you commit to incorporating the promises from John chapters 15–17 into your narrative base? (Here's an example. You might respond: "The next time I face X situation, I will remember what Jesus promised in John chapter . . ."

Focus Summary

The way we speak about our everyday situations reveals our narrative base. Often an examination of the way we talk about problems will reveal that our narrative base is made up of fear, worldly "wisdom" that is counter to what the Bible says, or other elements.

Fortunately, a narrative base can be changed! If you are operating out of fear, worry, or principles not found in the Bible, you can begin focusing on the promises of God and letting your language reveal to yourself and others that you truly believe those promises and are willing to operate on them.

Even if you have a narrative base that is Biblical, it can always be expanded. Remember that Rahab knew enough about the God of Israel's power that she wanted to ally herself with Him. But once she had a promise that she would be saved, it gave her greater courage and ability to hold on through difficult times. The same thing will happen to you if you increasingly incorporate trust in God's promises as you speak about the problems you face in life.

Chapter Five Response

Our technological society wants us to believe that the only things that are truly "real" are those things that we can access by either our own senses (sight, hearing, taste, touch, feeling) or by devices that measure things and events around us. If something can't be perceived through the senses (either our 0something) or quantified by measuring, then they're said to be not "real." Even in research done at the sub-atomic level where things can't actually be seen or even measured, scientists depend on measurements of the *effects* of such invisible objects such as quarks and neutrinos upon things they can see. Similarly, deep-space scientists talk about black holes and other phenomena no one has ever seen, but whose influence on surrounding stars can be measured.

The Bible contends that reality has two parts: the part you can see, and the part you can't see. It would have no argument with those who would say that our physical world is "real." However, the Bible teaches that God's unseen realm is not only just as "real," it should be more influential on our thinking than the physical world we live in.

Look at 2 Corinthians 5:1-5. What does this passage say about the relative importance of earthly struggles compared with the heavenly home that awaits us?

_____

_____

_____

_____

What is the "down payment" or deposit that verse 5 speaks of, which guarantees the promises of God?

_____

_____

_____

_____

How could the Holy Spirit be seen as a link between the unseen and the seen, according to these verses?

How could it be said that the red cord of Rahab functioned in a similar manner as the Holy Spirit functions in verse 5?

Read 2 Corinthians 5:6-10. What do these verses say is the relative importance of what we see compared to what we know only by faith?

What specific actions and words of Rahab show you that she lived by faith and not by sight?

What situation are you currently facing in which there is a conflict between what you see (and feel), and what Scripture says? (Hint: if you're having trouble thinking of a situation, ask yourself, "Where do I tend to lose hope in specific promises of God being fulfilled in my life?")

_____

_____

_____

_____

While it's abundantly evident that the promises of God are a great blessing and help us to hold on in difficult situations, it's also difficult to keep those promises uppermost in our minds when what we see around us would tend to make us lose hope. In other words, the words of God can bless, but they also test.

This was something that Joseph in the book of Genesis discovered. As a child, he received visions from the Lord that he would rule over his brothers. Those same brothers sold him into slavery and Joseph spent the next two decades of his life as a lowly servant or a prisoner in a jail. At that point, what he saw certainly didn't match up with what God had told him!

Read Psalm 105:7-22. How must Joseph's knowledge of the fact that God would eventually rescue him have helped him in difficult situations?

_____

_____

_____

_____

Similarly, Rahab's knowledge that she'd eventually be rescued must have served as a test for her as well. From these two cases of Joseph and Rahab—in which people believed the promises of God even when it seemed that the fulfillment of those promises was distant or unlikely—what can you generalize about the relative power of the unseen over the seen?

_____

_____

_____

_____

There are often great differences between what you see around you—the seemingly unresolvable difficulties you face—and what God has promised. In what way would it help you to see this great apparent discrepancy as a test?

_____

_____

_____

_____

Focus Summary

There's no way to "naturally" or automatically make a connection between what we see around us and the unseen realm of God's power. It is the words of God that say to us, in essence, "What you see and feel is real, but it's not the deciding factor in any situation. My will, My promises are what can change the reality you see."

The Holy Spirit, who supervised the writing of all Scripture,[103] is Himself a link between the unseen eternal realm and us who dwell in this temporal one. Without the Scripture, without revelation, we wouldn't have any way of knowing those promises!

Like the red cord of Rahab, His presence in our lives links us to those promises. His guarantee pervades our being as He indwells us and turns our eyes to the unseen.

Chapter Six Response

In Judges, the book that follows Joshua, all that God told the people would happen if they turned from Him did indeed occur. Time after time the people rejected God, and He turned protection away from them. Finally, the people found themselves for forty years in a political desert, where they had to live under the iron boot of the barbaric Philistines. As He had repeatedly done in recent years, the Lord prepared to raise up a leader for the people to free them from their misery.

Read Judges 13:1-3. What were the facts of Manoah's wife's ability to have children, as stated in verse 2?

_____

_____

_____

_____

_____

How did the *Angel of the Lord* represent what would happen to her regarding the birth of a child?

_____

_____

_____

_____

Read verses 4-5. What were the conditions placed on Manoah's wife?

_____

_____

_____

_____

Read verses 6-7. What did the wife of Manoah say to her husband that indicated that she believed the words the *Angel* had spoken?

_____

_____

_____

Read verses 8-17. What did Manoah say that showed he believed the *Angel's* representations of the coming fact of his son?

_____

_____

_____

Read verses 18-15. How did the wife use her confidence in the promise of God as a narrative base to logically reason that she and her husband weren't going to die?

_____

_____

_____

In what way did the representations from the *Angel* change the facts of Manoah's life and that of his wife?

_____

_____

_____

Think of a situation in which you are having trouble in focusing on the promises of God because of your fears. Look again at the way Manoah and his wife never used the word "if" but rather the word "when" in referring to the promise of a son. Now read John 14:1-4 and write below what you can expect when you contemplate your situation.

_____

_____

_____

_____

Read Isaiah 49:14-16 and write what you can expect.

_____

_____

The Old Testament prophet Daniel was once in a situation where he'd received a vision that terrified him because he didn't know what it meant. In fact, he became physically faint and fell down, he was so frightened. But an *Angel* was sent to him to explain the vision. Read Daniel 10:10-14. What can you generalize about the way God responds to our pleas for help?

1) Write a generalization about how God responds to people who are truly trying to figure things out with God's help.

_____

_____

_____

2) What do these verses tell you about whether or not your prayers for understanding are always going to be answered immediately?

_____

_____

_____

A large percentage of the Bible as a whole is prophecy. In what way is prophecy representation that precedes and forms facts?

_____

_____

_____

When Jesus spoke to anxious people, He had to remind them to overcome a "natural" tendency to worry. In fact, He had to command them not to worry! Read Matthew 6:25-34.

What representations of God of provision formed facts for the birds?

_____

_____

_____

What representations of God of provision formed facts for the lilies?

_____

_____

_____

_____

Why did the birds and lilies not need to worry?

_____

_____

_____

How does God's knowing what we need (His representations of our needs) lead to the formation of the fact of food, drink, and clothing for us?

_____

_____

_____

_____

Focus Summary

God has shared with us one marvelous aspect of His personality—the ability to represent facts. It was His creation of language that He put in us that distinguishes us from the animal kingdom, for we alone can not only represent facts with words, we can represent representations when we talk about words themselves!

He also shared with us another aspect of His personality—the ability to represent facts before they even exist. This is what He did in eternity, before the six days of Creation. Likewise, every writer, every artist, every woman who bakes a cake has a mental representation of the finished product before ever taking up pen, paintbrush, or baking pans. But whereas our creative abilities are limited by the fact that we are not omnipotent, God has no such limitations.

Whatever He "dreams up" and then promises to His people, no matter how extravagant or seemingly "impossible," He has the ability to make reality.

All it takes is just one word from Him, and reality changes to conform to that word.

Chapter Seven Response

With very few exceptions, all of the events of the Biblical past are accessible to us only by the linguistic representations as found in written form in Scripture. However, the exceptions to this are remarkable, and deserve a look.

Just by way of review, let's remember that *iconic* representations are those that are accessed by the senses—things we see, touch, smell, etc. On the other hand, linguistic representations are those ways that we communicate through speaking and writing. (Okay—it is true that part of accessing a linguistic representation is through sight or hearing; however, the linguistic symbol itself, by definition, is language-based.)

Read Genesis 9:8-17. What was the *iconic* symbol this passage speaks of, and what did it signify?

_____

_____

_____

_____

_____

Read Romans 1:18:20. Here God shows His justifiable distress against human beings who, for thousands of years, have seen visual *iconic* symbols of His power and His nature, and yet do not believe and actually suppress the truth about God. What does verse 20 say are the *iconic* —see-able— representations of His power and nature? (If you're having trouble answering this question, skip to the next one and then come back to this one.)

_____

_____

_____

_____

_____

Read Psalm 19:1-4. What does this passage say that God uses as a way of communicating information about Himself to people?

_____

_____

_____

_____

_____

Briefly state in your own words what this passage says we learn about God from the *iconic* representations we see in nature.

_____

_____

_____

_____

_____

Iconic representations, such as a rainbow or other feature of nature, while impressive to the mind, are not a complete source of information about God. What would the linguistic representations about Him as found in Scripture add to a person's understanding that a rainbow, for instance, couldn't convey?

_____

_____

_____

_____

_____

From what you've read about *iconic* representations, would you say that they are capable of telling a person the complete truth about what they represent if not accompanied by explanatory words? Why or why not?

_____

_____

_____

_____

Read Romans 6:1-10. This passage speaks of an act in which we are called to participate, an action that represents something beyond itself. What is that act?

_____

_____

_____

According to this passage, how does that act represent a past event or events in the life of Jesus?

_____

_____

_____

Read 1 Corinthians 11:23-26. In this passage, the apostle Paul is telling believers about the use of some *icons* to remember a past event.

What are the *icons*, or symbolic physical items, that this passage mentions?

_____

_____

_____

Write down some things that the physical act of eating the communion bread and drinking the cup convey to you personally.

_____

_____

_____

Focus Summary

God knows how we crave *iconic* representations. While the promises of His provision are helpful to us, there's nothing quite like the *iconic* taste of a good meal to make us really grateful for our daily bread. We know from Scripture about His power, but the *iconic* representation of the sound of a tornado brings it home. We can read about brotherly love all day long, but that *iconic* feel of a hug from a sister makes it real.

And yet, we know the *icons* are always just partial. You can't live just on bread, Jesus said, but on every word that comes out of God's mouth. In fact, if you have to choose between the bread and the words, only one of them can keep you eternally alive.

The stones by the riverbank were a powerful *iconic* symbol to subsequent generations that would be awed by the sight of large stones that once were in the middle of a raging river. But without the explanation of how they got there and what they meant, they were just a remarkable pile of rocks.

Today the pile of rocks may not even exist. But through the words of Scripture, we can access them and the event they represented as if they happened yesterday.

Chapter Eight Response

In Chapter Eight we looked at two significant concepts. One was the way that God has expected His people to take the impact of events of the Bible as if they'd happened to them personally. The other concept concerned the way that the events of the Bible are accurate: that is, they convey truth completely, in a way that secular history cannot. Let's look at some additional Scriptures to reinforce both of these concepts.

Read Deuteronomy 26:1-11. In this passage, Moses instructed the people before they crossed over the Jordan, telling them that the time would soon come in which they would enjoy the agricultural products of the new land. However, they were to look at those products not as just the end result of their own efforts, but to see them as gifts from God and thus accordingly to return a portion of them to Him.

How does verse 3 show that they would see the produce as the fulfillment of ancient promises to their forefathers?

_____

_____

_____

_____

_____

In what way do verses 5 and 6 show that God's people were to consider events that happened before the Passover as part of their own personal histories? (Hint: the "wandering Arameans" mentioned here were Abraham, Isaac, Joseph, and his brothers.)

_____

_____

_____

_____

_____

Explain in your own words the value of accepting as your own personal history such events as the Passover and the crossing of the Red Sea.

_____

_____

_____

_____

_____

In what ways would considering those things as part of your past be helpful to you?

_____

_____

_____

_____

_____

List any other stories in the Bible that you think would edify your faith if you saw them as manifestations of God's power as near and as accessible to you as the representations you have of your own past.

_____

_____

_____

_____

_____

The Holy Spirit, who superintended the selection of all the details of Biblical stories we read, was very precise in the choice of what details would be included in order to convey what God viewed as truthful, complete, and helpful to us. The Holy Spirit is more than just the omniscient Narrator, He is absolute arbiter of significance, and we can be assured that what is included is what we need to know. Let's look at two

familiar accounts in Scripture and see how this is true.

Read 1 Samuel chapter 17. What physical details about the terrain or setting of the battle are included? Why do you think this is so?

What physical details of description of the people involved are included? Why do you think these are included?

What does David say in verse 45 that show he understood that the power of linguistic representations would triumph over the iconic representations of power that he saw Goliath had?

From what you know about representations in general, why could it accurately be said that 1 Samuel 17 is more accurate than what David would have remembered about the killing of Goliath the day after it happened?

Read Luke 22:7-20. In this account, we learn that Jesus and His disciples ate a Passover supper that would have special meaning and would change the consciousness of His followers just as the Passover of old had done for the people of the Old Testament. Thirteen persons were present: Jesus, Simon Peter, Andrew, James, John, Philip, Bartholomew, Matthew, Thomas, James the son of Alphaeus, Simon the Zealot, Judas son of James, and Judas Iscariot. Note that Luke, who had "carefully investigated everything" (Luke 1:1-4) in order to write the account of the life of Jesus, was not among those thirteen.

Taking into account the role of the Holy Spirit as He moved on the minds of men as they wrote the accounts that would become Scripture, how could such a person as Luke, who was not an eyewitness of the Last Supper, have been able to give a more accurate account of the event than, say, the memories of the eyewitness Bartholomew as he recalled the event?

_____

_____

_____

_____

_____

Since all events are converted into representations for our minds to access, and since we cannot "get back into" the past of even an hour ago, how could it then accurately be said that we are as equidistant from the representations of our dinner last night as from the representations of Luke as he described the Last Supper?

_____

_____

_____

_____

_____

How could it be accurately said that no event of Scripture

is any more remote than any other, no matter how long ago that event happened?

_____

_____

_____

_____

_____

Focus Summary

The idea is hard to swallow, at first: that a source of information could be more accurate than our own experiences is difficult to accept.

But, of course, that is exactly what Rahab did. Just as Rahab was called upon to adopt God's representations of a past event as if it were her own, so we as believers must adopt the representations of the Bible as if they were our own.

Chapter Nine Response

As we have seen in previous mentions of the life of Jesus on earth, He wasn't impressed by anything but faith; He didn't play favorites except to honor even the most desperate person who trusted in Him completely.

We saw in Chapter Eight how often in history He has been involved in human situations. Whenever He appeared, whether in a pre-mortal theophany or in the flesh during His earthly life, He always reflected the character, personality, and aims of His Father.[104]

Read Hebrews 1:1-4. In what ways does this passage say Jesus reflects the Father?

_____

_____

_____

_____

In verse 3, when it tells of Jesus "sustaining all things by his powerful word," the word "sustain" is the Greek word for a continuous, dynamic action, not a passive posture. Now that we have seen how active Jesus has been throughout ancient history, what would you say this verse tells us about His involvement with us today?

_____

_____

_____

Read Ephesians 1:18-23. Here we learn of God's "incomparably great power." Who is this power for? What does this passage say that power "is like?"

_____

_____

_____

One of the great lessons that Joshua's encounter with "the commander of the army of the LORD" teaches us is that God has "the big picture" in mind in any situation. Write a brief generalization from Joshua 5:14, focusing on either 1) God's power or 2) God's ability to meet the needs of a believer.

_____

_____

_____

_____

_____

Read Isaiah 45:1-7. This message is one that Isaiah was to deliver to Cyrus, a pagan king that God would use to accomplish His purposes. In it, God expresses how He will use His limitless power. In what way did the battle of Jericho exemplify what is said about God in verse 7?

_____

_____

_____

_____

_____

Another lesson we can learn from Joshua's encounter with the Lord is that when God decides to do something to save the faithful, you'd better decide to get on board! Let's look at some Scriptures that show this.

Read Exodus chapter 14. When the angel of God who had been guiding the Israelites went behind them, the pillar of cloud did so as well. In what way did the pillar of cloud perform two functions at that time (verse 20)?

_____

_____

_____

_____

Similarly, how did the wall of water perform two functions?

_____

_____

_____

_____

Read Isaiah 8:11-15. This passage shows that our decision to follow God determines how He relates to us. In Rahab's day, in what ways did God prove to be both a snare and a sanctuary to the people who crossed the Red Sea and to their children?

_____

_____

_____

_____

_____

Read Luke 2:21-35. From what you know about the way people reacted to Jesus during His earthly ministry, how would you say that the prophecy of Simeon in verse 34—about how Jesus would cause the rising and falling of many, and that He would be a sign that was spoken against—was fulfilled?

_____

_____

_____

_____

_____

Focus Summary

To this point, we have studied many examples of the tenderness and vulnerability of God toward His people of faith. But Joshua's encounter with the *Angel of the Lord* is a sobering reminder of other aspects of our God. He's often a

God of mystery. He's no pushover and won't be manipulated by us but remains instead resolutely focused on the welfare of His people. He's also enormously powerful, with entire angelic armies at His disposal as well as mastery over the forces of nature and even time itself.

In the case of the crossing of the Red Sea, we see that the same pillar of cloud could illuminate one side and actually cause darkness on the other. The Egyptians had seen the same plagues and miracles as the Israelites and could have made a decision—go with the people that God favored. But they didn't, and their position behind the cloud of separation meant they would die in the Red Sea that the Israelites had just crossed dryshod.

He is often mysterious and terrifying, this God we serve; and we should never forget those aspects of His personality. Rahab understood this, and unlike the Egyptians, she resolved to risk all to be on the lighted side of His presence.

Chapter Ten Response

In Chapter Ten, we looked at various aspects of persuasive faith as exemplified by believers throughout the Bible. Here are some more examples.

Persuasive faith sticks to its guns about what it knows to be true. Read Acts 4:1-35. Previously, in Acts 3, we read that Peter had healed a crippled man. But ultimately, why were Peter and John put into jail?

_____

_____

_____

_____

What was the "point" of Peter's answer to the rulers and teachers (verses 8-12)?

_____

_____

_____

In verses 19 and 20, what did Peter and John say was the basis for their actions?

_____

_____

_____

_____

How did the courage of Peter and John affect the leaders (verse 13)? How did their persuasive faith affect the other Christians?

_____

_____

_____

During difficult times, persuasive faith recounts God's mighty deeds of the past. Read Psalm 77. List things from verses 1 through 9 that show the psalmist's discouragement.

_____

_____

_____   _____

_____

_____

There is a turning point in his thinking in verses 10-12. What is it?

_____

_____

_____

_____

Verses 13 through 20 describe the same historical event that had impressed Rahab. What is that event?

_____

_____

_____

Think of a troublesome or discouraging situation you are facing. How can recounting to yourself and others the mighty deeds of the Lord help you to re-represent your present situation?

_____

_____

_____

Persuasive faith doesn't dictate an outcome for any situation, but can commit to faithfulness no matter what happens in the end. Read Daniel chapter 3. How did Shadrach, Meshach, and Abednego verbalize faith in God versus their faith in a certain outcome?

_____

_____

_____

_____

_____

What was the result of the three men's persuasive faith upon Nebuchadnezzar?

_____

_____

_____

_____

Write a generalization from verses 16 through 18.

_____

_____

_____

_____

Think of a situation you are facing which has an uncertain outcome but in which you know you must verbalize your faith to those who are watching you as you handle the situation. Write below some of the characteristics of God you have learned as you have studied the Bible.

_____

_____

_____

_____

In what situations in the coming week could you talk about those characteristics of God and your faith in Him to those who are watching you handle the situation?

_____

_____

_____

_____

_____

Focus Summary

The passage in James 2:14-26 is one we have covered before, one that equates the faith of Rahab with the faith of Abraham (who is without a doubt the greatest example of faith mentioned in the Bible). But this passage emphasizes more than just faith, it emphasizes that faith is never invisible—it is always accompanied by works. In other words, faith acts.

But just as true is the fact that *faith talks.* There is no such thing as silent faith. It can't help itself—it has to be shared.

We don't know what words Rahab used, we just know they did the job and kept her family inside her house. Her faith acted, talked—and won the lives of everyone she loved.

Chapter Eleven Response

Rahab's faith not only saved her, it saved everyone dear to her. But there's a flip side to examples like that. The consequences for our lack of faith and trust in the character of God are appalling—not only in the cost to ourselves but to innocent victims around us. Take the children of the unfaithful Israelites: Some were born just a year or two into the desert journey, and spent the first four decades of their lives on manna and spring water because of what their parents did. Even the two faithful adults, Joshua and Caleb, wore the same clothes and shoes they took out of Egypt, and ate the same food as everyone else. But those who hadn't sinned got to see something the unfaithful never lived to witness: the miracles of the crossing of the Jordan and the taking of Jericho.

In the following two examples we see how people faced the prospect of disaster. Notice, as you read and respond, how the unseen power of God did miracles for people who expressed their faith in Him.

Read 2 Chronicles 20:1-30. What was the seemingly-impossible situation that King Jehoshaphat faced (see especially verses 2 and 12)?

_____

_____

_____

_____

_____

How can we see that he exercised persuasive faith?

_____

_____

_____

_____

We are not told what kind of weapons his army had. What was the basis of the strength of the army? List below verse numbers and some information for these elements:

1) Prior promises of God

2) An appeal to God's sense of justice

3) Humility and appeal to God for help

What significance do you see in the fact that the front lines of the Israelite army were singers? What did they sing about?

Who fought the battle?

_____

_____

_____

_____

What was the result of the battle?

_____

_____

_____

_____

From this passage, write a generalization about the power of God when believers face real danger.

_____

_____

_____

_____

Read John 11. What questions did Mary and Martha have about the fact that Jesus had waited so long to come?

_____

_____

_____

Why did Jesus say to His disciples that He was glad He hadn't been there before Lazarus died?

_____

_____

_____

_____

What did Jesus say in verse 40 that would be the result of belief in Him?

_____

_____

_____

_____

There were two types of reactions to the raising of Lazarus from the dead. What were they?

_____

_____

_____

_____

Write a generalization from this passage about why God sometimes waits to act in our behalf.

_____

_____

_____

Jesus gave Mary an opportunity to state her faith in Him. Is there a situation in your life where you feel that God has waited to respond to your requests? Write a brief statement of your faith in Him even though you have not had an answer to what you've asked. Then take this statement of faith to Him in prayer each day next week.

_____

_____

_____

_____

Focus Summary

Often our lives look chaotic and out of control, and the actions of God seem circular and meaningless to us. Jehoshaphat and Mary and Martha learned that trusting Him and expressing faith in His protection and love bring blessings.

Rahab, too, learned that you can't interpret events without God's explanations for them, His representations of His enduring care and constant attention to the details of our lives. We just can't survive mentally or emotionally without that.

But when we fail as individuals in our faith and trust in God, we can take comfort in the fact that we are part of a kingdom of which He is the head. In fact, the Bible describes the collective of believers—His church worldwide—as His bride, who waits for His return someday.

For 2000 years we have waited for Him. For over 104,000 Sundays, we have proclaimed His death, and celebrated His resurrection. Surely our persistence as a people in doing that, our determination not to let any generation drop the ball, but to continue—surely we can take some encouragement that He has allowed us to prove (at least to ourselves and to others in the world) that we *can* wait in hope.

Chapter Twelve Response

What is a generalization?

_____

_____

_____

_____

_____

From your study of the life of Rahab, write a generalization about:

God's view of a sinful past

_____

_____

_____

_____

The meaning of security

_____

_____

_____

_____

The actions of God that seem unproductive or meaningless in your life

_____

_____

_____

_____

The importance a Christian should put on God's mighty deeds of the past, as seen in the Bible

_____

_____

_____

_____

_____

The importance of *icons* or *iconic* actions such as baptism or eating the Lord's Supper

_____

_____

_____

_____

_____

How God looks at needy, desperate people when they ask Him for help

_____

_____

_____

_____

_____

Persuasive faith of the type practiced by Rahab

_____

_____

_____

_____

_____

Further review:

What is a fact? What is a representation?

_____

_____

_____

_____

Give an example of a representation of a fact that God has given in the Bible, and contrast it to a "natural inclination" you might have to provide a different representation of the same fact.

_____

_____

_____

_____

What is the area in which you have the greatest tendency to reject God's representations of facts in your life?

_____

_____

_____

_____

What have you seen in the life and words of Rahab that would give you some clues about how to handle the problem of correctly representing the facts of your life?

_____

_____

_____

_____

In what way do Biblical representations save us when facts can't?

_____

_____

_____

_____

_____

Can you give an example of this from the life of Rahab? From your own life?

_____

_____

_____

_____

_____

Focus Summary

I don't know about you, but I can't wait to meet Rahab in eternity. Let's make a covenant of the red cord. Let's all learn to risk as she did, hope as she did, love as she did.

Notes

Part One

Chapter Two

1. Deuteronomy 1:19-35
2. Genesis 18:16-33
3. James 2:25
4. Luke 3:23-37
5. Genesis chapter 38
6. 2 Samuel chapters 11 and 12
7. Luke 7:36-50
8. Mark 7:24-30
9. Ruth 2:2-3
10. Jeremiah 39:15-18
11. Ephesians 2:12-13
12. Zechariah 3:4
13. Hebrews 10:17
14. Romans 8:28
15. 1 John 1:7
16. 1 Peter 2:24
17. Micah 7:18-19
18. Hebrews 8:12
19. 1 Timothy 1:15-16

Chapter Three

20. Hebrews 11:31
21. Exodus 1:17-21
22. 1 Kings 22:19-28 and Jeremiah 38:24-28 are other examples of lying that don't seem to be condemned, but in these two passages there is no indication that the one telling the lie was actually commended for doing

so; as were Rahab and the Hebrew midwives.
23. Romans 13:1-5
24. Acts 4:19; 5:29
25. Most of our information about the events during that 40 years is taken from the book of Numbers and from Deuteronomy. Numbers chapter 20 seems to indicate that "the first month" mentioned there and its subsequent events are those that took place during the final year of the desert experience.
26. Numbers 33
27. Numbers 21:21-33
28. Numbers 21:1-3
29. Numbers 31:7-12
30. Numbers chapters 22-24
31. Numbers chapter 26
32. Numbers 20:2-13
33. Numbers 21:4-9
34. Numbers chapter 34
35. Numbers chapter 25
36. Numbers 14:33-34
37. Exodus 14:22

Chapter Four

38. Matthew 12:34
39. Genesis 18:16-33
40. Exodus 32:30-34; Deuteronomy 9:11-29; 10:10
41. Isaiah 38:1-6
42. 1 Samuel 1:1-20
43. Judges 6:1-40
44. Mark 6:6; see also 7:24-30; Matthew 8:10; 15:21-28; Luke 7:9, mentioned later
45. Genesis 24:14
46. Exodus 3:12
47. 1 Samuel 14:6-10

Chapter Five

48. Matthew 15:21-28
49. Exodus 12:13, 22-23

50. Ephesians 1:7
51. Colossians 1:20
52. 1 Samuel 4
53. Acts 17:24-27
54. Romans 8:24
55. Hebrews 6:19
56. Hebrews 11:1

Chapter Six

57. Exodus 15:13-17
58. Numbers 14:9, *King James Version*
59. 1 Samuel 14:6
60. Leviticus 26:3-13
61. Leviticus 26:14-39
62. John 1:1, 14

Chapter Seven

63. The only exceptions were the tents of Joshua and Caleb, who alone had believed that they could take the land.
64. Joshua 4:22-24
65. Deuteronomy 1:19-40
66. There is actually a third type of representation, one that we have dealt with briefly in the chapter about Rahab's red cord. That third type of representation is the index, or linking representation. The cord, while admittedly serving as an iconic representation of the words of the spies who promised to return, also served as a link to the future when those promises would be fulfilled. As also mentioned in the chapter about the red cord, the Holy Spirit functions as such an index or link, bringing the representations of God to the material world. Some examples of this linking or index function are seen in the birth of Jesus (the plan of God that became reality through the agency of the Holy Spirit as depicted in Matthew 1:8) and the writing of Scripture, where the Holy Spirit brought the thoughts of God to men who wrote them down (1 Peter 1:20-21).

Chapter Eight

67. Rahab the harlot was not the only person to bear the name Rahab in the Old Testament. (Similarly, we know of several Josephs and Joshuas, for instance.) Rahab was also an Old Testament name for Egypt. Perhaps Isaiah's sense of humor and knowledge of Rahab the harlot would have influenced his tongue-in-cheek reference to Egypt as "Rahab the Do-Nothing" in Isaiah 30:7.
68. See Genesis chapter 34, especially verse 25, for a description of a battle waged against a city of men who'd been incapacitated by circumcision.
69. 2 Corinthians 4:17

Chapter Nine

70. Read the account in Exodus 3 along with Acts 7:30-34.
71. Genesis 15:17
72. Read the following: Exodus 13:21; 14:19; 23:20-23, along with Isaiah 63:9.
73. See, for instance, the way the word "angel" is used in Revelation chapters 2 and 3 as a designation for the messengers to the seven churches of Asia Minor.
74. For instance, Jesus asserted this truth in John 6:46.
75. Just as Jesus accepted both the title of God and the worship of His followers on this earth, as seen in John 20:24-29.
76. Hosea 12:4 refers to this incident and calls the being an angel, which would be in keeping with this entity being the angel of the Lord.
77. Matthew 13:36-43; 2 Thessalonians 1:6-10
78. Revelation 13:8

Chapter Ten

79. Malachi 3:14-18
80. John 14:1-12
81. Genesis 3:6
82. Mark 8:34-36

83. Mark 8:38
84. Luke 8:14
85. Numbers chapter 25

Chapter Eleven

86. As none of us can understand what we see around us—the facts of our lives—without the verbal representations of God to tell us how to interpret them.
87. Deuteronomy 2:1-3
88. Deuteronomy 1:30-33
89. Genesis 18:3-8; Judges 6:11-18
90. Hebrews 10:13
91. Matthew 24:36-51

Chapter Twelve

92. John 20:24-31
93. Colossians 1:17
94. Deuteronomy 29:11-15
95. Deuteronomy 4:29
96. Deuteronomy 10:19
97. Matthew 24:21-22
98. Hebrews 11:33-34
99. Matthew 22:34-39
100. Judges 2:6-15
101. 2 Chronicles 16:9; Lamentations 3:22-24

Part Two

Chapter Response Introduction

102. James 1:22-25

Chapter Five Response

103. 2 Peter 1:20-21

Chapter Nine Response

104. John 5:16-30

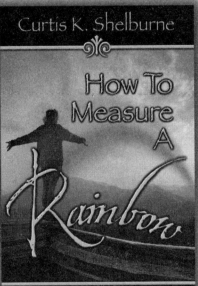

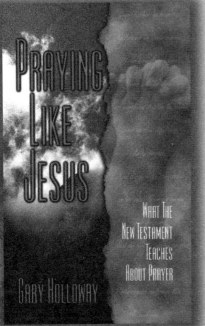